THE Beast IN YOU!

A WILLIAMSON *KALEIDOSCOPE KIDS*™ BOOK

DEDICATION

To Deanna, Kara, and Macky, my own lovable beasts.

Library of Congress Cataloging-in-Publication Data

McCutcheon, Marc.
    The beast in you : activities & questions to explore evolution/by Marc McCutcheon; illustrations by Michael Kline
        p.   cm.
    "A kaleidoscope kids book."
    Includes bibliographical references and index.
    Summary: Explores the facts and questions of human evolution through hands-on activities, crafts, and experiences.
        ISBN 1-885593-36-8 (alk. paper)
    1. Human evolution Juvenile literature. 2. Human beings—Animal nature Juvenile literature. [1. Evolution.] I. Kline, Michael P., ill. II. Title.
GN281.M245   1999
599.93'8—dc21   99-20855
                    CIP

Kaleidoscope Kids™ Series Editor: **Susan Williamson**
Design: **Joseph Lee Design: Kristin DiVona, Joseph Lee, Sue Yee**
Illustrations: **Michael Kline Illustration**
Photographs: **Gianni Dagli Orti/Corbis,** cover; **John Reader/SPL/Photo Researchers, Inc.,** page 49; **New York Times Co./Archive Photos,** page 68; **Archive Photos,** pages 73,75; **Heck's Pictorial Archive of Nature and Science/Dover Publications, Inc.,** page 40
Printing: **Quebecor Printing, Inc.**

Printed in Canada

Williamson Publishing Co.
P.O. Box 185
Charlotte, Vermont 05445
1-800-234-8791

10 9 8 7 6 5 4 3 2 1

THE Beast IN YOU!

ACTIVITIES & QUESTIONS TO EXPLORE EVOLUTION

Marc McCutcheon

Illustrations by
Michael Kline

WILLIAMSON PUBLISHING • CHARLOTTE, VT

CONTENTS

A Look in the Mirror
5

Spot the Animal!
6

Ch-Ch-Ch-Changes!
21

The Science of Evolution
30

Our Early Hominid Ancestors: Lucy & Friends
39

The Family Album: A Step Toward Humankind
55

Getting Closer to Us!
70

We're Here! Modern Humans & Our Evolving Future
80

From Ape People to Humans: An Annotated Time Line
90

Museums to Visit
92

Bibliography
93

Index
94

A LOOK IN THE MIRROR

Look in a mirror. What do you see? (Besides one handsome kid!) Look closely. See a beast? No, of course not. Look again. See *parts* of a beast? Hmm? Smile. *There's one!* Hold up your fingers. *There's another!* Wiggle your ears. *There's another!*

Would you believe that whenever you're afraid or angry, an ancient beast springs into action? Yet it also lies quietly with you when you sleep. Sometimes the beast is warm and fuzzy. But sometimes it is as ferocious as a lion.

Who is this weird creature, and why can only *remnants*, or parts, of it be seen? Where did the beast come from in the first place? And why has most of it disappeared?

Well, to find some answers, or at least the answers as scientists and researchers know them today, you're about to embark on an exciting adventure deep inside you and far, far into your distant past. How far? Oh, most of it took place not that long ago. Say about 5 million years ago (which is recent in geological time). But some of it took place as long as 10 million years ago, when your ancestors lived very differently than you do now.

Shall we begin?

SPOT THE ANIMAL!

You are a human being. So is your mother, your father, and all of your grandparents and great-grandparents, and all of their parents and great-grandparents before them.

But if you go back through your family history, say, to your great-great-great-great-great-great-great-great-ancestors from 10 million years ago or more, you won't find a human being. You'll find that dear old, *ancient* Grandma was an animal — an animal with a thick coat of hair and an incredible talent for climbing trees.

Actually, you and I are animals, too. But we're different from the beast your grandmother from 10 million years ago was. We don't walk on all fours anymore. Nor do we bite (baby brothers and sisters excluded). Or hoot and growl (baby brothers and sisters excluded again). But we *do* carry dozens of reminders of what we used to be.

Find a mirror where you can get up close. We're going to play a game called Spot the Animal.

LET'S SEE A BIG SMILE!

Found a mirror? Great! When you first peer at your reflection, it may be hard to see anything that resembles a ferocious beast. After all, you're rather friendly-looking, right? But wait. Look more closely. And *smile!*

If you're like a lot of people, you'll notice a set of pointy teeth just on the sides of your four middle front teeth. One on the right, one on the left. Top and bottom. Like Count Dracula! Or your average beagle.

In fact, these teeth are called *canine teeth*. (Don't worry if you can't see yours clearly; they're not as noticeable in some people as in others.) Canine teeth have stronger roots than other teeth. And they're usually longer and sharper. But why?

Roots

Do scientific terms and names sometimes seem as difficult to remember as a foreign language? Well, guess what? You are right on! Most scientific terms are either completely foreign, or they have foreign roots as a basis for them.

All plant and animal life have *genus* and *species* names in Latin or Greek (like *Tyrannosaurus rex*). Other words, like *zoology*, for example, have Latin or Greek roots, too (zoo + logy = "animals" + "study of").

"Canine" comes from the Latin word *caninus*, meaning "dog." And, if you've ever seen a dog growl, you know where the name "canine teeth" came from. So, when you look for your canine teeth, think doggy teeth, and you'll spot that animal immediately!

CIRCUS

NOV. 5-12

CIVIC CENTER

Back in the time of our early ancestors (when these teeth were much bigger), canines were used for defending against attacks from rivals and predators and for shredding tough vegetation. They were also used on occasion to kill other animals for meat. That may sound ghoulish, but in the old days, supermarkets and McDonald's didn't exist. Food had to be found or hunted.

Animals who still hunt for a living (like lions and tigers) have huge canines. The roots of these teeth are unusually deep, making them almost impossible to pull out while tearing into raw flesh.

So, canines were not only sharp for good shredding, but also had deep roots so they'd stay put. Not a bad invention for scavengers and hunters.

In humans, canine teeth are called *vestiges*, or a *vestigial element*. A vestige is a body part our ancestors needed in the past, but that we no longer use (or use very little) today.

Notice any other vestiges in the mirror?

Get the Bite on Canines

The next time you're having your teeth cleaned, take a look at your dental X-rays to see how long *your* canine roots are.

THE ULTIMATE VESTIGE

Medical journals occasionally record human infants who are born with tails (that are then surgically removed). A tantalizing clue to our beastly heritage, if ever there were one!

LOOK FOR THE REASON

Ostriches can't fly. So why do they have wings?

Go back far enough in ostrich history and you'll find a much smaller bird that *could* fly. The ostrich has traded the advantage of flight for the advantage of size. Its wings, then, are only vestiges. (Birds taking up residences on islands without predators can actually lose their wings, sometimes in as little as a few thousand years.) Vestiges provide clues to the kind of beasts we all once were.

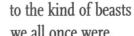

Grins and Grimaces

Back to that mirror. Really *grin*. Nice and wide now. Now think about how a dog looks when it's angry and threatening to bite. The muscles in its face pull back and wrinkle. Its teeth are revealed and menacing. It's a look designed by nature to *scare* you into running away.

Which is exactly what *your* smile *used* to be.

In prehistoric times, a smile was not a friendly greeting at all. It was, in fact, the most important part of a *snarl*.

Snarls actually helped our ancient ancestors avoid fights, because the sight of one's canine teeth was sometimes enough to frighten rival animals away. On your next trip to a zoo, watch a baboon yawn. That yawn with canines showing is a subtle form of threat, much like the snarl.

Today, of course, a smile is welcoming. Incredibly, it now tells others that you're nice — the complete opposite of its original meaning!

Think About It!

Grrr! Welcome!

How did threatening snarls turn into welcoming smiles? The beast in us tells us that it has always been a response acknowledging another's presence — once negative and now positive.

Do you think it gradually became a way to acknowledge another's presence when our ancestors *didn't* feel threatened? So, instead of being menacing, the snarl became smaller and canines weren't shown. Like, "Hi! I see you. I won't bother you, so don't bother me."

Does a smile signal welcome in all human cultures around the world? Ask your friends from other cultures if smiling has always been "the nice thing to do."

THE BETTER TO SMELL YOU WITH, MY DEAR

Are you beginning to see the beast in you? Hold up the mirror (yes, again), and take a close look at that little divot above your top lip and below your nose. Notice the slight depression — like a trough — running up and down?

That's also a vestige. It's called the *rhinarium*. Millions of years ago, our rhinariums were moist strips of flesh that helped our ancestors to smell. Animals with moist snouts, such as dogs, still have rhinariums, because the sense of smell is much more important to them than it is to humans.

Wolf-Speak

In the story *Julie of the Wolves* by Jean Craighead George, an Eskimo girl lost in the wilds learns how to speak the language of the wolves — especially how they actually grin to avoid fights.

Notice the body language of other animals. How does your dog or cat show you that it is angry, frightened, or glad to see you?

Ears to You!

Can you wiggle your ears? Some people can.

The ability to wiggle the ears is a throwback to a time when animals (like dogs) could *cock* or adjust the ears to aid in hearing. The structure for ear-cocking is gradually disappearing. In fact, the majority of us can't move our ears at all. But like most vestigial elements, ear muscles will probably remain in some family lines for thousands of generations to come.

KA-CHUNK!!
PSSHAHH...

DOG FOOD

Don't stop now! Hold up your hands and look at your fingers. Can you guess what your fingernails evolved from?

If you said *claws*, give yourself a round of applause.

Although our ape-like ancestors had nails much like the ones we have today, some of our earlier ancestors sported claws to defend themselves from predators and, sometimes, from each other. Today our "claws" are gradually disappearing. Beyond scratching an itch, we simply don't need them anymore.

The Evolution Solution

THE GREAT APPENDIX MYSTERY!

So, snarls and wiggly ears are vestiges of times when survival needs were different.

What else are we carrying around that we don't need? Take a look inside. Know anyone who had an appendix removed? How is it that people get along just fine without it? A vestigial element! The appendix, a small, worm-shaped organ in your lower abdomen, serves absolutely no function.

Some scientists believe it may have been part of an ancient digestive system for strange foods. Others think it may have helped fight infections. But no one is really sure what it did. And, only humans, some apes, and wombats have appendixes! It's one of those mysteries of evolution waiting for someone like *you* to solve.

Crazy Claws!

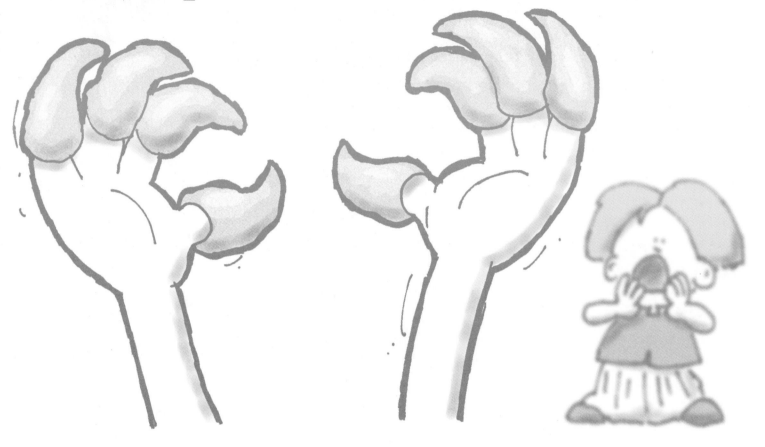

What was it like to have claws instead of fingernails? Our early ancestors knew. And if you let your fingernails grow too long, you'll know, too — from mistakes at the computer keyboard to a not-so-great piano lesson. Long, clawlike fingernails get in the way of our manual dexterity (our skill and ease in using our hands).

Get close to the beast in you by making clay claws. Simply poke your fingers into a soft mound of clay or Play-Doh. Curl your hand a bit, and shape the clay into claws. Let dry, and then wear them around the house. Try doing some thoroughly human things like tying your shoelaces, holding a toothbrush, or unwrapping a granola bar.

So what's the verdict on claws? Useful (other than for scaring little sibs) or a vestigial element from those beastly days when we were walking on all fours?

(When you're done wearing your claws, take a needle and thread, and string them together into a necklace. Wear this for a day, and you'll know what the height of cave-people fashion was!)

The "Plucked Goose" Defense

Claws and canines were vital defensive weapons in our ancient ancestral days. But they weren't our only defenses.

Try this for a "you-were-there" experience. Open the door to your freezer, and stick your arm in for a moment. Feel the chill? Does your arm's skin look like a plucked chicken — er, goose, that is? (You can pull your arm out now.)

Could goose bumps be part of your beastly body's line of defense?

Goose bumps, quite simply, are the body's way to erect the thick coat of hair *we once sported*. Raised hair provides added insulation, which means more warmth. Because we have no heavy hair, all we see when we're cold now are the goose bumps created by tiny muscles called *erector pili.*

If you've ever seen a dog or other animal on a frigid winter day, you may have noticed that the hair on its back was standing on end. Erector pili at work!

Sometimes, when you're very frightened, the tiny hairs on the back of your neck will stand up. You feel it as a chill.

That chill was once important. Triggering the erector pili muscles, it raised our ancestors' *hackles* (hair on the back of the neck and back), making their bodies look larger and therefore more ferocious to their enemies.

You can still see this reaction whenever a cat and a dog meet face-to-face for the first time. The fur on their backs stands at attention immediately! Sometimes this defense works so well that both animals are frightened away at the same time!

Oh look, honey, school starts Monday!

GREAT!!

"...I Felt a Chill Run Down My Spine..."

Now you know where this saying came from! After all, when you feel a spine-tingling chill, you have a heightened sense of danger, right?

These "sayings" are a great way to begin a scary story. Next time you and your friends are sitting around at night or having a sleep-over party, turn out the lights, sit in a circle, and start an eerie chain tale (where each person adds to the story). Your ancestors would approve if you were sitting around a campfire, too! And, for special effects, pass around a flashlight that the speaker holds under her chin.

How scary is this tale? Well, did your "hair stand on end"? Did it "give you goose bumps" or "get your hackles up"? Would you call it "a hair-raising experience"? When you are all thoroughly frightened, turn on the lights and just "chill out"!

FIGHT OR FLIGHT?

Next time you're very frightened, take your pulse to count how many times your heart beats in a minute. (See text at right.) You'll notice that it beats much faster when you're scared, even if you're lying perfectly still.

Why? It's called the *fight-or-flight response*. When you are frightened, your heart goes into emergency action in case you need to fight off a ferocious beast or quickly run away. More blood pumped to the right muscles helps make you stronger and quicker.

The fight-or-flight response is still your body's way of preparing itself to face danger. Throughout life on earth, this response has probably saved millions of animals from being eaten! Today, we humans face different dangers, but it continues to protect us by keeping us alert and ready to act in any emergency.

Test Your F-or-F Response

For most kids ages 8 to 12, the typical resting heart rate, or pulse, *is around 90 beats per minute, but normal rates can range anywhere from 70 to 110.*

To take your resting pulse, place two fingers over the arteries in your wrist. Feel your heart rate? Count the number of beats in exactly one minute. Now, run up a flight of stairs a few times. Check your pulse again. What's the difference? That's your fight-or-flight response in action!

Bare Naked?

Goose bumps beg the question: Whatever happened to our hairy coats, anyway?

Why are humans, um, well, *naked*?

Actually, humans *aren't* naked. Truth is, scientists say we have pretty much the same number of hairs as apes. That's right! The difference is that now most of our hair is very thin and short. Therefore, it's harder to see.

To Have or Not to Have — Hair, That Is!

Hair. We love it in some places, hate it in others. Many American women shave their legs and underarms. Many European women don't. Men love hair on their chests, but more often than not, hate it on their backs and in their ears. Can you guess how most people feel about nose hairs?

Look around. A remnant of our once-thick hair can still be found on our heads and on the underarms of most adults, and on the faces and chests of most men. (Look at some of the men on the beach this summer. You'll notice that some are more *beastly* than others.) The fine hair that covers much of our bodies is called *vellus*. The hair on a gorilla (called *terminal hairs*) is, by contrast, thicker.

There may be any number of reasons why the human coat thinned over the centuries — to help keep the body free of icky bugs and parasites, for example. Bare skin, quite simply, is much easier to keep clean than fur.

Hairless skin is also easier to cool in hot, sunny climates, where we originally evolved. And who knows? Bare skin may simply have been more attractive to members of the opposite sex. Whatever the reason, over millions of years, humans lost their thick coats.

It all comes down to how *natural* we want to look. What's natural, you ask? Why, untamed like an animal, of course!

Here is something to ponder: Why do women tend to shave their legs and underarms, but men don't? Is that some sort of "vestigial" sexist commentary that says men should appear beastlike and strong, while women should look weaker and less able to protect themselves? Could it be we need to *evolve* a little more in our thinking?

WHO, ME? ANGRY?

Finally, we end the game of Spot the Animal with one last mirror image.

Get right up close to that mirror and make the angriest face you can. Pretend you're so mad you could spit tacks!

Pretty scary, huh?

Ever wonder why humans get angry?

Imagine an animal in the wild that *never* got angry. Imagine, especially, a young animal that did not have a temper. Imagine that no matter what you did to this animal, it simply would not become cross. What would happen to it?

It would probably starve to death or be eaten. Without the threat of a bad temper, rivals would steal all of its food or attack it. So, the ability to get angry was actually a good thing. Sometimes.

Although nobody likes temper tantrums, the anger impulses handed down from our ancestors remain in our brains. Some of these feelings are much stronger and are triggered much more easily in some than others. Sometimes they get humans into trouble. As civilized beings, of course, we can *control* the animal instincts still in us. With our high intelligence, it is always possible to find peaceful ways to vent our ancient rage response (see next page for some ideas).

A HAIRY COINCIDENCE?

Incredibly, hair can also be seen on the human fetus inside the womb. At six-months' development, the fetus grows a downy coat of hair called the *lanugo*. It drops off before birth, or shortly after. Is this a clue to our beastly past, or do you think it is merely a coincidence?

Keeping Cool When Your Ancient Animal Anger Surfaces

Your brain — the highest form of animal intelligence — tells you to walk away from the group taunting you on the corner, or from your brother who is having a temper tantrum. But your anger impulse draws you closer to a nasty confrontation.

Here are five things to help you keep your cool when the heat's turned up:

Take a few deep breaths. *Use this time to "dilute" your anger.*

Put some distance between you and the problem. *Walk on the other side of the street, or go get a glass of water at home.*

Change the dynamic. *Add others to the environment by "attaching yourself" to a group of people ahead of you (even if you don't know them), or calling a friend if you are at home.*

Use your smarts. *Think about what is best for you in the long run, not about how you'd like to "get even" now. Later, plan how to avoid these situations.*

Redirect your energy. *Anger and fear can be helpful, just as they were in beastly days. They alert you to your feelings. Now, do something positive (one step at a time) to change things for the better!*

The Big Snooze

You sleep an average of 8 to 12 hours most nights. Think it's wasted time?

Why can't we simply stay awake all the time?

Answer: Sleep may be yet another vestige from our past.

Many sleep experts believe the big snooze evolved to protect animals and to help conserve their energy at night. Think about it: What changes if you're up all night?

➤ *You burn more calories.* That means you must find more food, which in the wild can be difficult and dangerous.

➤ *You increase your risk of a serious injury.* With limited night vision, you may blunder into a hole and break your leg, or poke out your eye on a low-hanging tree limb. You might even fall off a cliff!

➤ *You increase your risk of being seen, heard, smelled, found, and devoured by a saber-toothed tiger, leopard, or hyena.* Uh-oh! Not that!

Sleep, then, may have forced us to lie still for our own good. If you don't move, you don't need to eat — and *you* won't be eaten!

Of course, some animals sleep during the day and come out at night — a reverse survival strategy that works to their advantage.

Do a Sleep Survey

Lots of kid-adult arguments revolve around sleep: when to go to bed and when to get up. But you probably know that.

Ask about six kids and six adults about sleep. Here are some possible questions to get you started.

◈ *How many hours a night do you usually sleep?*

◈ *Do you wake up feeling rested or still tired?*

◈ *Do you wish you could stay up later at night? Sleep later in the morning?*

◈ *Do you think of yourself as a night owl or an early bird?*

◈ *Are you late for school or work a lot because you can't get up in the morning?*

◈ *Does physical exercise make you more sleepy or more alert?*

◈ *Do you think sleep is a waste of time?*

Compile your results (a bar graph works well), and see what you learned about our human sleeping habits. Do you think our sleep patterns are vestiges in our evolution, or do you think they are a necessary part of human development?

CH-CH-CH-CHANGES!

Now that you've seen some beastly vestiges in wonderful *you*, you may be wondering exactly who *you* are and where *that beast* came from.

Ask a friend to name the animal you most closely resemble. He'll most likely say an *ape*. An ape? No insult intended — it's simply a fact. Apes look like us. We look like apes. Should it be any surprise that humans are distantly related to apes?

Actually, scientists believe humans *evolved*, or developed, from humanlike creatures that had evolved from the apes. But before we take a look at the evidence close-up, let's consider what it means to *evolve*.

What exactly is this thing called *evolution*, anyway?

NECESSARY ADJUSTMENTS

Over thousands, even millions, of years, animals and plants often change to better fit their environments. Giraffes may develop longer or shorter necks, depending on how high off the ground most of their food is. Elephants may grow larger or smaller, depending, among other factors, on long-term food supplies. Other animals may develop thicker coats if their climate grows colder.

But these changes usually only happen over *many generations* of animals. In some cases, it can take millions of years. The evolution of humans and most other animals doesn't happen quickly. (Germs and bugs, though, are another story! See page 27.) Nor can any animal change, or evolve itself, or its children. (Humans, however, can and do tinker with their health and with the health of their offspring, which ultimately alters the course of evolution.)

Newfoundlands and Dachshunds

To understand how much an animal can change or be changed by its environment, consider dogs. We humans have bred them into a vast array of shapes, sizes, and colors. Big ones. Small ones. Long-snouted ones. Flat-snouted ones. Fluffy ones. Short-haired ones. Barky ones. Silent ones.

Some dogs are so unlike each other that to a person from another planet, they would appear to be completely *unrelated*. (Think of a small Dachshund next to a huge Newfoundland!) In a very short 10,000-year span, we have created (from the wolf) a whopping 200 different breeds of these animals.

If 200 *different* kinds of dogs can come from a *single* ancestor, would it be so hard to believe that a human being could develop from an *ape*? Especially in a time span of not 10 thousand years but *10 million!*

Maybe you can bring yourself to believe that such a thing in nature is possible. For now, let's assume you can (more debate about this later). But even so, you still must have that one important question you'd like answered:

> *How? How could an ape possibly evolve into a human being?*
>
> The answer, in part, is **small changes over long periods of time.**

A Coat of Many Colors

Imagine you're a hare in summer. Life is wonderful! Your brown coat helps you blend into the dry, brown grass around you.

By blending in with your environment — called *camouflage* — you're almost impossible to see. If a coyote or a hawk can't see you, you don't get eaten! *It's a simple law of nature.* You will survive to mate with other hares, which will then produce more baby brown hares.

But think for a minute. How would a brown coat protect you in winter? A brown coat in white snow would make you much *easier* to see. And that means you'd be spotted and eaten by hungry predators much faster. Not a good situation, for sure.

The evolution solution? *Develop a coat of fur that turns brown in the summer and white (or partially white) in the winter.*

And that is exactly what mountain hares have evolved to do, over *many thousands of generations*. When cold weather comes, their brown coats turn partly snowy white, providing a perfect camouflage. When the warmth of spring returns, those white coats turn brown once more.

These animals, then, have made an adjustment to fit more perfectly into their environment.

Now, turn the tables one last time. What would happen if, because of a climatic change, it didn't snow anymore and the hares' coats continued to turn white anyway? Over many generations, these animals would gradually die out (because they would be easy prey), to be replaced by other hares that had coats that stayed *brown* all year long! Quite amazing!

Hare Hide-and-Seek

Try this. Draw a large rabbit on each of three sheets of white paper. (Don't worry, they don't have to be great works of art!) Color one rabbit brown. Color another one yellow. Color the last one white. Cut out each rabbit.

Tape each rabbit, one next to the other, on the trunk of a tree. Step back at least 50 feet (15 m) — about five times the length of your room. Imagine you are a hungry coyote. Which

one of the three rabbits can you see best, and, therefore, which one is most likely to end up as your dinner?

If there is snow on the ground (or use an old white sheet), place the rabbit pictures on the ground and back up 50 feet (15 m) again. Now which one can you see best?

If you were a rabbit, what color would best help your chances of survival?

Thank Goodness for Accidents

A hare's "smart" coat could only develop with what scientists call a *mutation*, or an accidental change. As strange as it sounds, nature actually designs some plants and animals to have these built-in mutations occasionally. They can affect everything from what color an animal might turn out to be, to how well it sees, or how fast it can run.

Most mutations are of no benefit — or are even harmful. But every now and then one comes along that *helps* an animal. In our hare's case, it was a little accidental spot of brown on the hare's fur that *stayed* brown all year — a spot that would be passed down to that hare's babies and to their babies' babies, and so on. If the hares with the biggest brown spots survived better (because of their better camouflage), their offspring would grow increasingly brown as the centuries passed.

This is evolution at work, making *small changes over long periods of time.*

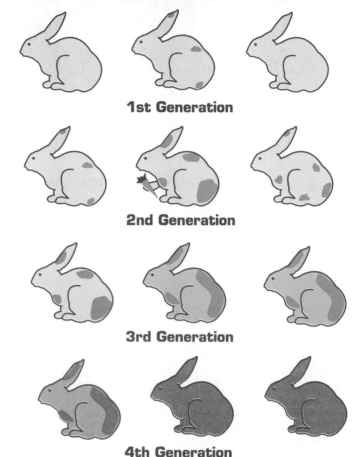

1st Generation

2nd Generation

3rd Generation

4th Generation

The Evolution Solution

ALL IN THE FAMILY

We can see natural variations in a species just by looking at ourselves — some helpful, some bothersome. What physical traits do you see that run in your family? "Bad" lower backs? Big feet? Flat feet? Long legs? Poor eyesight? High cholesterol? Unusually long noses? (Some things, of course, are not about evolution; they are just family preferences or habits that are passed on to kids, such as enjoying reading or loving Italian food.)

One of the best ways to see physical traits is to look at old photos of earlier generations and ask senior family members about physical strengths and weaknesses. Can you figure out when a trait first showed up in your family?

Then, try to decide whether these natural variations are helpful or not (assuming you were in a struggle for survival of the fittest, that is). Hmm …

CHECK MY COAT

Mountain hares change their coats, but what about polar bears? Their coats tell a whole different adaptation story. You see, polar bears aren't really white. Yes, they certainly do look white, but that's because the center of each of their long outer hairs carries light that filters out through the sides, making the dark inner hair appear white.

And that's good news for the bears! The dark hair carries sunlight right down to the polar bear's black skin, which then *absorbs* the sun's heat. If its hairs were really white, its coat would *reflect* the sun's rays and heat, and the bear might freeze in the terrible arctic cold. If their coats looked dark-colored, however, polar bears would be much more noticeable, and they'd lose the advantage of surprise when sneaking up on seals, their prey.

The polar bear's wonderful *adaptation* to its environment gives it the best of two worlds — it can stay warm and catch its prey, too. It's a pretty smart evolution solution, don't you think?

DEADLY CHANGES?

In less than 30 years, more than 200 species of insects have adapted to be able to resist the deadly insect poison DDT. This means these insects have all changed in ways that now protect them from being killed by that poison. Chemical companies know that insects can adapt quickly, because insects breed so many generations in a short time span (see page 29). That's why scientists are continually inventing new poisons.

It's the same story with rats. They, too, have evolved to resist the poison (Warfarin) originally developed to kill them.

Ditto, germs. They evolve even faster than bugs or rats! Many medicines (especially *antibiotics*) invented years ago to keep bacteria that cause hard-to-cure infections in check are now ineffective.

Like bugs and rats, these supergerms are always evolving to meet the challenges of their environments. It's the microbial version of the survival of the fittest!

A MATTER OF TIMING

There are a lot of terms used to mean change when we talk about evolution. The differences in their meaning have a lot to do with time span, degree of change, and how large a group it is happening to. And, oftentimes, some terms are used interchangeably.

Evolution: Small changes, or *adaptations,* over thousands and even millions of years that gradually result in a new species of animal or plant. Humans *evolved* from ape-like ancestors over millions of years.

Mutation: An accidental change in the genetic structure that may be harmful, neutral, or sometimes beneficial, to an animal or plant. If it is beneficial, the mutated animal or plant may survive through *natural selection*.

Adaptation: A small change in response to a change in environment or climate, such as the mountain hare's changing coat. The creatures that survive by adapting to their environment continue the larger process of evolution.

Extinction: When a species of a plant or animal no longer exists on earth. Their population is zero. Many species that once populated the earth are now extinct.

Take *All* Your Medicine

When your doctor prescribes an antibiotic like amoxicillin for your ear infection, sometimes you feel better in a few days, but you have to take the medicine for a full 10 days. Why do you need to take it for so many days? Hint: Think about those bacteria that got to taste your medicine but are still alive.

Go Figure

A *generation* is loosely defined as a group of people or animals all about the same age. A grandmother, a mother, and a daughter are three generations. You and your friends of about the same age are one generation. Your parents and their friends are another generation. Your grandparents are yet another generation.

A generation, more specifically, is the average number of years an animal or plant lives before producing offspring. In humans, this number is around 25. In rats, a generation is about 60 days. In fruit flies, a generation is only 10 days! (Species that regenerate so quickly cause humans some very serious problems. See page 27.)

So, in 1,000,000 (one million) years, how many human generations are there? In one year, how many fruit fly generations are there?

A Multi-Generation Photo

How many generations can you gather together? It doesn't have to be of one family. Take a snapshot of the most generations you can assemble in one place. Is it four? Five? For example, how about someone who is in his or her early twenties (1), with an infant (2), a parent (3), a grandparent (4), and a great-grandparent (5)? Great photo!

[Answers: 40,000 generations of humans; 36.5 generations of fruit flies.]

30

THE SCIENCE OF EVOLUTION

Given enough time, small changes can eventually produce a subspecies or an altered form of an original animal.

By taking advantage of its special adaptations, the subspecies may then out-hustle the "original" animals, forcing them into extinction.

But sometimes both original and "sub" continue to live side by side, each taking up its own ecological niche. (Humans, for example, evolved from ape-like ancestors, but the apes did not die out.) Thus, life on earth has evolved from just one type of single-celled animal to more than 10 million different species of multi-celled plants, insects, birds, fish, reptiles, and mammals. Wow!

Drive Slowly — Whale Crossing!

Sometimes, over millions of years, animals change to the point where they become *different* animals altogether. As incredible as it sounds, whales were once animals that lived on *land*. Vestiges of leg bones can actually still be found inside their huge, blubbery bodies!

Many land-oriented animals spend a great deal of time in the water, and they, too, may evolve into permanent swimmers, just as the whale did. Otters, hippos, and sea lions are just three animals that appear to be in between evolutionary stages.

A Whale of a Picture

If today's whale is the end result of millions of years of the evolutionary process, what do you suppose its prehistoric ancestors looked like?

Use your descriptive talents in a painting, a sculpture, a scientific drawing with labels, or in a descriptive history to "flesh out" your image of the evolution of a whale from land to sea.

What changes would have to take place for your land mammal to become an aquatic one? **Hint:** *Fossils of whales from 55 million years ago show they didn't have blowholes at the top of their heads, but they did have nostrils in the front!*

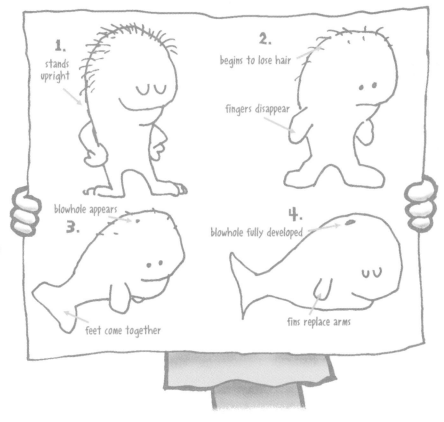

1. stands upright
2. begins to lose hair / fingers disappear
3. blowhole appears / feet come together
4. blowhole fully developed / fins replace arms

neigh!

The Dino-Bird Connection

Believe it or not, birds are thought by many scientists to have evolved from — of all things — dinosaurs!

Scientists recently uncovered two turkey-sized species, *Protarchaeopteryx* (pro-ark-ARP-tuh-riks) and *Caudipteryx* (cod-IP-tuh-riks), whose fossils show the clear impressions of down, feathers, and jagged teeth. These new discoveries now join the famous fossil of the *Archaeopteryx* (ark-ay-OP-ter-iks), a reptilian bird with a lizardlike tail, in helping to prove the dino-bird evolution.

Because they are usually too delicate to be preserved, feathers rarely show up in fossils. Thus, they may have been much more common than the fossil record actually reveals. Even *Velociraptor*s, those awful, slashing dinosaurs in the movie

Whoa, Nellie!

Horses and elephants, too, have undergone dramatic changes. We know from the *fossil record* (the history of once-living things and climatic changes preserved in fossils) that horses were once very small. Go back into the past far enough, in fact, and you'll find skeletons of fully grown horses only a foot (30 cm) tall! Imagine *that* ride!

Jurassic Park, may have had their own colorful plumage, according to some scientists.

But feathers aren't the only evidence we have of the bird-dino connection. Indeed, birds share many traits with dinos, including the same breastbones, wishbones, three-toed feet, and swiveling wrist joints.

Need more convincing?

Take a close look at the next ostrich you see. You may, in fact, be looking at the great-great-great-great-great- (multiply by roughly a few million here) granddaughter of a *Tyrannosaurus rex!* As astonishing as it sounds, at least one scientist is now saying that even the most terrible dinosaur of all time, the mighty *T. rex* herself, may have sported feathers!

The Evolution Solution

A MOUTHFUL!

Are you evolving? You bet! The human brain is growing.

To make more room for the brain, the jaw is *shrinking*. Modern-day humans — like you and your friends — now have too many teeth to fit comfortably in their mouths. So, for most folks, soon after the last set of molars, known as "wisdom teeth" (because you are such a wise guy), come in, they have to be pulled out!

$E=mc^2$

How Life Is Evolving Around Us

Take a close look at the natural world around you. Can you see evolution at work?

◆ ***Flippers or flight?*** Scientists think the flippers penguins use for swimming were once wings used for flying. Why do they think that? Because penguin's bones are hollow. All flying birds have hollow bones that are much lighter, an adaptation designed only for flight.

◆ ***From laying to stinging.*** Did you know that only female wasps can sting? That stinger now used to attack you evolved from a specialized egg-laying organ, only on females, of course.

◆ ***Snake legs?*** That's right! Boa constrictors still have remnants of hind legs and a pelvis, evidence that they were once lizards. (One fossil of a snake from 100 million years ago actually has rear legs!)

◆ ***Blinded!*** Moles and cave salamanders have the remnants of eyes that can no longer see. But don't worry. They live in the dark, so they don't need eyes anymore.

◆ ***Disappearing teeth.*** Why would baby anteaters grow a row of teeth that vanish before birth? Scientists think sometime in their distant past, anteaters ate something other than soft ants and termites. That something required teeth for tearing and gnashing. The fetal teeth that develop and then disappear are only a ghostly vestige. Fetal whales also grow teeth that disappear at birth, evidence that they, too, once had a very different diet.

THANK YOU, CHARLES! (DARWIN, THAT IS)

That animals (and humans) can gradually change to better fit into their environments was first discovered and written about by a very famous scientist named Charles Darwin. A naturalist who lived in the 1800s, Darwin described evolution as a kind of natural selective tendency allowing only the fittest to survive. His books *The Origin of Species* and *The Descent of Man* describe in detail how animals and humans evolved from the early ages of prehistory.

Darwin discovered that although some animals stay the same over time (sharks and turtles are almost exactly the same today as they were millions of years ago, for instance), many others undergo changes in order to compete better in their surroundings.

His scientific observation is something simple, yet almost nobody had noticed it before him:

➤ *Animals who find the most food and stay alive the longest have the most children.*

➤ *Animals who can't find enough food and die young produce fewer or no children.*

Eventually, if no offspring survive, the entire species will die off, or become *extinct*.

What Darwin observed seems obvious to us now. Unless animals can adapt to their surroundings and keep pace with other animals in finding food and producing healthy young, they will eventually disappear from the earth — permanently.

**Charles Darwin
1809–1882**

All in the Family

Do you share any interests with members of your family? Kids, parents, and grandparents often do activities together, as a way for kids and grown-ups to share time and ideas.

Charles Darwin was no different than most of us as kids. He came by his interests in science and nature quite naturally. His grandfather Erasmus Darwin was a naturalist, physician, and a poet, too! His grandfather even believed there had been some kind of evolution of living organisms, but he never explored it more deeply.

Do you think Charles Darwin and his grandfather talked about evolution together? Perhaps. But one thing we do know is that Charles Darwin was aware that his views would be unacceptable at the time. That's one reason he wanted to research *how* evolution actually happened; he wanted to break new ground in the science of biology based on *facts* supporting his *observations*.

Going ... Going ... Gone!

Extinction is what happens to a whole species or group of plants and animals that fail to adapt to changes in their environment. In fact, 99 percent of all creatures that ever lived are now extinct, or they have evolved into different animals!

Think of it — 99 out of 100 animals that ever lived are now gone. *Forever.* To show just how many that is, take 100 pennies or 100 beans and put only one off to the side. This is the only survivor!

Animals and plants face extinction from many sources. Viruses or infections, diseases, predators, human consumption, loss of natural habitat, and extreme competition for limited food sources can all combine to eliminate a species from the face of the earth forever.

CATASTROPHIC EVENTS!

Many creatures become extinct after a major change in climate. Earth has undergone many drastic climate changes over the course of millions of years. Some were triggered by volcanoes spewing massive amounts of smoke and debris into the sky, blocking out sunlight and cooling the land.

The extinction of the dinosaurs 65 million years ago is thought to have been caused by a giant asteroid (rock from outer space) crashing to earth. It sent up huge plumes of smoke that enveloped the land for years, killing plants and the animals that ate them.

And the ice ages brought long periods of arctic cold as far south as present-day New York and London. Though the ice ages weren't sudden events like asteroids, they took huge tolls on habitats and those species that lived in them.

BRRRR...

Think About It!

The Elephant's Trunk

Fifty-five million years ago, the ancestor of the elephant had only a fat upper lip. No trunk. Can you think of any reasons why the elephant developed its trunk? Ask yourself how a trunk might help the elephant survive. What can an elephant do with a trunk that it couldn't do with a plain old nose?

With a trunk an elephant can:

Here Today, Gone ... in the Next Million Years?

Change is an ongoing event. Sometimes we can make educated guesses about future changes (smaller jaws, for instance) with some degree of accuracy, and sometimes our guesses — even if based on observations — don't hold up over time.

Take a good look at yourself. What else might be in the process of changing in humans? Think about how we work and play, eat and sleep. Any ideas about what we may need more of and what we could do without in the year 30,000?

To get you started, consider: Why are our baby toes and pinkies so small? And why are our thumbs shaped differently than our other fingers? Are these changes on the way in (meaning that in the evolutionary future we will be "all thumbs") or on the way out?

◇ **Pick up objects as large as a log or as small as a blade of grass.**

◇ **Reach up higher into trees for edible leaves and fruit.**

◇ **Suck up water without kneeling down.**

◇ **Give itself a cooling shower.**

◇ **Spray its back with dust or water to rid itself of parasites and bugs.**

◇ **Trumpet an alarm.**

◇ **Wrestle or greet peers.**

◇ **Give affection to its young.**

◇ **Smell water or a thunderstorm from miles away.**

Don't forget to wash behind your ears...

Moving *Back* Through Evolutionary Time

Knowing how useful an extra limb (like the elephant's trunk) can be, imagine that you're an animal minus a limb — you with only one arm, for instance.

For an entire afternoon, tie one of your arms behind your back and do everything with one hand. Try peeling a banana. Try hanging from a tree limb chimp-style while eating a banana (gotcha!). Try carrying several items at once over a long distance. Try wrestling with your kid brother or sister.

Not so easy! And, that's just the beginning. Now tie both arms behind your back and see how much you can do. Could you survive in the wild with no arms?

Believe it or not, our ancient ancestors did just that. What have thankfully evolved into our arms were once our front legs *several million years ago!*

OUR EARLY HOMINID ANCESTORS: LUCY & FRIENDS

Between 5 and 7 million years ago — not very long ago in geological time — some groups of apes living in Africa gradually began to change to better fit their environment (evolution continuing its work). Scientists think the changes came about because the forest where the apes lived had very gradually been changing into open grasslands.

When animals take on new characteristics, it is almost always because the land they live in has undergone some alteration. A wetland turns into a desert. A thick forest into an open grassland. And so on.

At first, the adjustments in the apes were minor. But as the forest thinned more and more, the apes were forced to find food on the ground.

Some of these animals had an awful time and were attacked and eaten by predators. (If you were out to lunch, you *became* lunch.)

Others couldn't find enough nourishment on the ground and starved. (The picky eaters, perhaps?)

A few — maybe because they were just slightly smarter, or stronger, or more willing to experiment with new food — survived.

These better-adapted apes had children, who took on the same adaptations as their parents. More and more, the old-style apes, who didn't or couldn't adapt, began to die off, while the new-style apes grew in numbers.

Over time, the new-style apes changed even more. These changes helped them to survive even better on the ground.

Among the most important of these changes?

The ability to stand and walk upright.

IS MORE ALWAYS BETTER?

Imagine you're one of these newfangled apes. Think about how the ability to stand on two legs might help you survive. Up on two legs, you can, for the first time, peek over tall grass to see when lions are sneaking up on you. That gives you a few more seconds to run and save yourself!

With hands free, you can pick up food and carry it over long distances. No longer are you limited to what you can carry in your mouth.

You can also use your hands to signal friends (think of the emergency hand signals for *Go back!* or *Shhhhhh!*) and maybe to even talk with one another. (Chimps in the wild use hand signs to communicate "Come with me," "Please groom me," "You're welcome," "May I pass?" and more.)

As critical as an upright posture was, however, it may not have been quite as important as one other development during this period:

Bigger brains!

BRAIN POWER

By examining ancient skulls, scientists know our ancestors gradually developed bigger brains. They found that, in general, the older the skull, the smaller it is. The closer to humans we get in time, however, the *larger* it is. Larger skulls mean larger brains.

The advantage of greater brain power is obvious. With brighter minds, these apes could *plan* and *organize*, perhaps even work as a *team* with assigned tasks. They could outsmart their strongest competitors — and better avoid those lions, tigers, and hyenas that would have them for breakfast!

These smarter apes lived longer and they lived better. And their survival brought about the evolution of even larger-brained apes. (Nature will keep on doing what works.)

These apes weren't quite human, but over many centuries, they became more humanlike. Scientists call these humanlike creatures *hominids*.

Brain Versus Brawn

It's easy to see how brains historically win over brawn (physical strength) just by looking at human domination over animals today. Big teeth can kill in a single chomp. And fast legs can help you catch prey.

But big brains do much more. In our ancestors, growing brains brought about the development of:

➤ better "friendship" skills
   ("I'll help you if you help me");

➤ more organizational power
   ("You guys gather plants and berries, while we go hunt for meat");

➤ the ability to plan far into the future
   ("Let's eat some now, and save some for later");

➤ an increasing dexterity (skill) with the hands
   (ideal for hurling stones and sticks at a rival or predator and for making crude tools).

But are there times when pure strength or a finely tuned body is more valuable than a quick-thinking mind and problem-solving skills? Which would you rather have as your survival skill in our world today?

WIMPS RULE! (Sometimes!)

Imagine a school of nine small fish living in a pond with one very hungry giant fish. When the giant fish swims near, three of the smaller fish always flee and hide behind a rock. A second group moves away but stays in the open. The three remaining are the tough guys. They bravely swim wherever they darn well feel like, no matter how close the big fish gets. Which group do you think lives the longest?

The toughies get the most food because they're not afraid to steal it from others. And they'll swim in scary places to find more food. The middle fish, on the other hand, get a fair amount of food, but not as much as the toughies. They like to play it safe. The scaredy-cats probably get the least amount of food of all. Perhaps they play it too safe by hiding and swimming away from danger all the time.

Does that mean it's always best to be brave?

Well, surprisingly, a real-life study of fish in a pond with a hungry predator showed that the timid scaredy-cats tended to live the longest. *Scaredy-cats rule!* Why? Because the braver fish got eaten! In a different environment, though, it is sometimes the brave animals that live the longest. And sometimes it is the animals in the middle that survive.

When there is a mix of personalities like this, an animal group (species) is much more likely to survive, no matter what the environmental conditions.

Now you can see why nature produces humans with so many variations. And so many personalities!

Hello, *afarensis*!

Sometimes hominids are called "ape men" or "cave men." But these names are not quite right. Only a small number of hominids ever lived in caves. And, of course, an equal number of hominids were women and children. So much for "cave" "men"!

One of the first of the hominids emerged around 4 million years ago (see time line, page 90). It is called *Australopithecus afarensis* (aw-stral-o-PITH-uh-kus aff-uh-REN-sis). That tongue twister actually means "southern ape of the Afar," named after the place in Africa where its bones were originally found.

Afarensis stood about 4½ feet (1.5 m) tall. It had a smaller brain and a larger jaw than a modern human. And it was, without pumping iron, as muscular as the typical professional wrestler is today.

How do we know that about an animal that lived so long ago?

It, like many other creatures, left behind its *fossils*.

But I Saw It!

Myth: Cave men fought, killed, and ate dinosaurs.

Fact: Even though you may see the cave people and dinos together in movies, humans and our prehuman ancestors were not alive during the time of the dinosaurs. The last of the dinosaurs died out about 65 million years ago. Our prehuman ancestors walked the earth around 60 million years *later!* It's not likely they'd run into each other in the neighborhood!

CLUES TO THE PAST

Fossils are remnants of living things preserved in rock. When an animal dies, it is almost always quickly eaten by scavengers. In rare cases, though, a dead carcass may escape a scavenger's notice. (Kind of like the dried-up tuna sandwich that "fossilizes" behind the living-room couch, where nobody can see it.) This might happen if the animal's body is carried away by water, such as in a flood, or falls into water and is buried quickly by *sediment* (sand, mud, and plant matter that settles to the bottom of water).

In these instances, the flesh rots away, leaving only the bones. Under the right conditions, the bones are *infiltrated* by minerals from the ground; the minerals get right into the bone and actually *take the place of it*. These minerals make the bones hard as rock. And then these hard bones may lie in the ground for millions of years.

Paleontologists (see page 54) can often guess how old a fossil is simply by examining the ground it came from. If the fossil is pulled out of an old layer of sediment, the fossil itself is very old.

Think About It!

Science Detectives

If you like solving puzzles, you'll like being a science detective. A lot of scientific and historical work involves thinking like a detective: *questioning, observing, hypothesizing, testing,* and *drawing conclusions.* It's like a gigantic puzzle with most of the pieces missing. So you need a good imagination and a lot of curiosity. It's so fascinating that — watch out — it might be habit-forming!

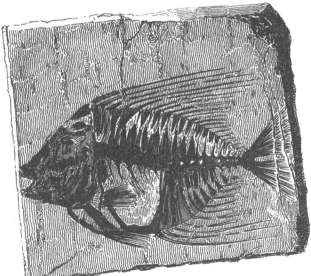
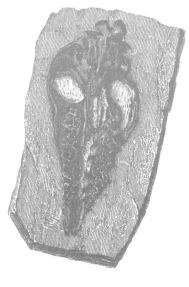

Fish and shell fossils of the Tertiary period, 66 to 1.6 million years ago.

Taking a Core Sample

Ask a grown-up's permission to dig a hole in your backyard. How many different-colored layers of dirt can you identify? Depending on your location, you may find anywhere from one to four different kinds of dirt: about 6 inches (15 cm) of dark soil on top, a layer of lighter, sandy dirt beneath it, and perhaps a bed of golden or reddish dirt beneath that.

Or, you may find only heavy clay.

These layers are much like the hardened sediment layers geologists study and measure to figure out how old a piece of ground or rock formation is. (In general, the farther down you dig, the older the ground.) Once they figure out how old a piece of ground is, they can then guess the age of fossils in it.

If you can't dig a hole, you may be able to take a core sample, *just like a geologist does:*

1. *Remove a small portion of grass, roots, and rocks from a small area of soft ground.*

2. *Find a length of strong pipe about 2 to 3 inches (5 to 7 cm) and drive it into the ground with a hammer. (Not too far, or you'll have trouble pulling it out again.)*

3. *Is the pipe full of dirt when you pull it out? Push the dirt out by inserting a narrow stick and tamping or pushing hard. Be careful: You're trying to keep the core of dirt in one piece.*

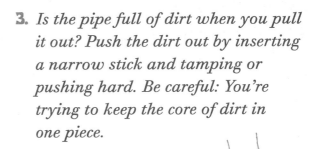
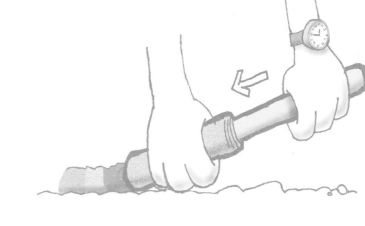

4. *Lay the core out on the ground and note any differences in color or texture. (Words to the wise: Getting a core sample is very difficult if you have heavy clay soil or pure sand.)*

5. *If you get a chance, take core samples elsewhere in your town, or when you visit a friend in another state. (Always ask permission first.) You may want to sketch each one. What kinds of differences are you discovering?*

Observations & Conclusions

A scientist who hunts for and studies hominid fossils is called a *paleoanthropologist* (PAY-lee-oh AN-thro-POL-uh-jist). (Say that three times fast!)

Paleoanthropologists uncovered the first skeleton of *Australopithecus afarensis* in Ethiopia, Africa, in 1974. By examining the sediment layer it came from, they guessed that this particular creature had died about 3.2 million years ago.

At first, nobody knew who or what the bones belonged to. They certainly didn't fit any known ape. Nor were they human. They seemed, in fact, to come from something *in between.*

By careful study of the fossils, the scientists thought that the skeleton probably belonged to a female. Why? They surmised this by the size and shape of her pelvis, the bones at the base of the spine. A female pelvis is usually wider than a male's, to create a wide birth canal.

Once assembled, the skeleton stood only 3½ feet (1 m) tall. That means when alive the creature probably weighed no more than 60 pounds (27 kg). Yet she wasn't a child. Scientists knew she must be at least 20 years old, because they could see her wisdom teeth, which only emerge during the late teen years.

The scientists nicknamed this little ape-person "Lucy."

Lucy & You

Find a light-colored wall or door and measure 3½ feet (1 m) up from the bottom. Mark this spot with a pencil dot. Now, stand next to the dot and mark your own height. Are you taller than Lucy was as a full-grown adult? How much taller than Lucy do you think you'll be when you're 20?

Jon 4½'
age 9

— LUCY 3½'
age 20

— FIDO 1½'
age 4

Meet Lucy!

Lucy had a large jaw and large teeth, but her small skull held a brain only one-third the size of our own! And, unlike us, Lucy could probably not speak anything more than a grunt.

Like all early hominids, Lucy probably had hair covering most of her body. And she was most certainly dark-skinned as well. In sunny, hot regions of the world, such as Ethiopia, skin pigment is darker to help protect the body from the harsher rays of the sun. (Light skin evolved much later, when hominids moved to northern regions of the world, where the sun is far less intense.)

Lucy had short legs with noticeably long arms and hands. With this chimpanzee-like build, she could probably scramble up trees with great speed and agility. But she came down from the trees often to hunt for food, to drink, and perhaps to explore. *And when she did, she frequently, if not always, did so on two legs!*

How did the paleoanthropologists know this? Lucy's leg bones tell the story! Like the leg bones of other upright-walkers (like you), Lucy's are thicker than those of four-legged walkers. Think about all the extra weight an upright-walker's two legs must carry.

Scientists also looked at Lucy's pelvis, which is shaped differently than a four-legged animal's. And they looked at her knee joints, which is a design only found in upright-walking humans.

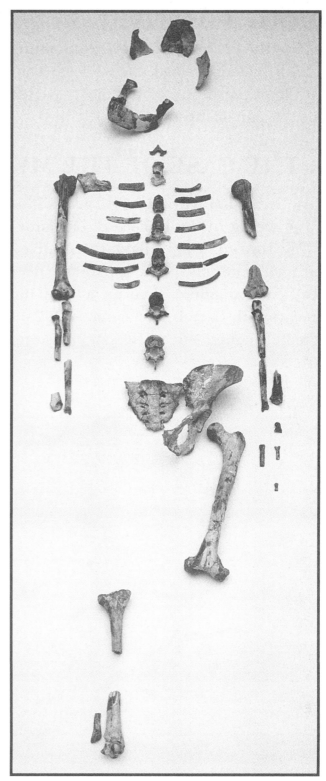

The bones of Lucy show she walked on two legs!

PROOF POSITIVE!

Despite the evidence, not everyone wanted to believe that Lucy and her friends walked on two legs. The proof came just a few years later, with one of the most spectacular fossil finds of all time. (A pair of Reeboks? No.) It was ...

... THE CASE OF THE MYSTERIOUS FOOTPRINTS

Andrew Hill dived on the ground to avoid being hit by a piece of elephant dung thrown by his friend. (You'd dive, too!) The two scientists (who apparently needed a break from digging) were on a fossil-hunting expedition in Laetoli, Tanzania, in 1976. By an incredible coincidence, Hill saw an astonishing sight as he fell:

A trail of humanlike footprints stretching for nearly 80 feet!

After careful study, Hill learned that the footprints belonged to none other than two members of *Australopithecus afarensis*, fellow Lucy-ites!

You see, millions of years ago, a volcanic eruption had covered the region in a layer of ash. When a rainstorm thoroughly soaked the ash, it turned into something similar to wet cement. When the two members of *afarensis* walked across the wet ash, their footprints hardened, and they were eventually covered up. It took centuries of harsh weather to uncover the footprints again — some 3.6 million years later!

One set of prints are quite a bit larger than the other. A mother and child? A male and a female adult?

Nobody knows for sure. But the tracks prove that *afarensis* did *not* walk like a chimp on its rear feet and front knuckles. Why is this so important? Scientists are always trying to figure out — even today — which of our ancestors got around on two legs first. (It's that competitive human thing!)

Do the Knuckle Walk

The thing about Lucy is that she had short legs and long arms — perfect for walking on all fours, so her two-legged stance was a surprise. Like chimpanzees today, some of our earliest ancestors (before Lucy, perhaps) may have walked on their knuckles. Find a soft carpet and try to walk on your own knuckles. Ouch! It's not as easy — or as painless — as it looks! What could evolution change about your body to make knuckle walking easier and more natural? (Hint: Think about your legs and arms as compared with a chimp's.)

Make Footprint Casts

Well, your footprint casts won't be 3.6 million years old, but knowing how to make a cast is good practice should you ever come across a great fossil find. (And it does happen!)

Create a plaster footprint cast (yours, a friend's, or even an animal's or bird's) just like a paleoanthropologist in the field. Scientists often make casts of fossils and footprints when the originals can't be removed from their sites.

Tools & Supplies

- Cereal-box cardboard
- Tape
- Large, clean can (a coffee can works well)
- Plaster of paris (from a hardware store)
- Container of water
- Garden trowel (or other small digging tool)
- Old toothbrush

1. Bend the cardboard into a collar-shape around the footprint. Fasten the ends of the collar with the tape.
2. In the can, mix $1\frac{1}{2}$ parts of plaster with 1 part water. Stir. The final consistency should be like gravy or pancake batter. Do the mixing quickly — plaster hardens quickly.

3. Pour the plaster over the footprint, making sure it fills the print completely. (A little overflow is okay.) Wait 30 minutes.

4. *When the plaster has hardened, carefully dig around the cast and remove it from the ground. Clean the cast, using water and a toothbrush.*

5. *You now have the reverse of the actual footprint. If you'd like to have the actual print, you can make a second cast. Just coat the cast in dishwashing liquid to keep the second cast from sticking. Then, repeat steps 1 through 4 with the collar at least 1 inch (2.5 cm) higher than the cast.*

Note: Please don't pour any leftover plaster down the toilet or rinse out your can in the sink. (It will clog them.) Just wrap the can in newspaper and throw it away in the trash.

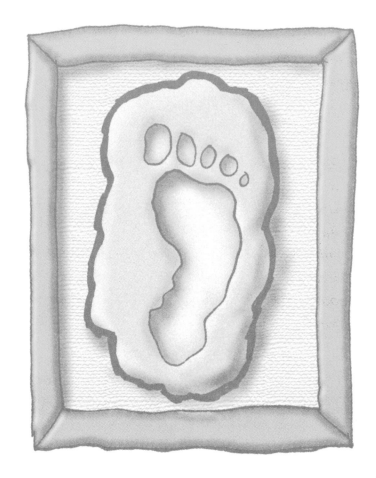

Who Does What?

Paleontologist, geologist, anthropologist — who are these people and what do they do?

For starters, they're curious people, just like you. They enjoy the aspect of science that tries to *understand* the present and *predict* the future by uncovering the secrets of the past. Many are scientific sleuths, piecing together a picture from bits and pieces of hard evidence.

Anthropologist: A scientist who studies the origin, culture, classification, races, physical characteristics, and social customs of humans. Anthropologists help us understand where ancient peoples lived and where groups of people live today; what they like to do, and eat, and wear; what tools they use; what they do for fun; and how they live every day.

Paleoanthropologist: A scientist who searches for and studies prehuman and human fossils. Paleoanthropologists help to identify the fossils like Lucy and *Homo sapiens* (modern humans like you!).

Paleontologist: A scientist who studies the life of past geological times (like when trilobites or dinosaurs lived)

through fossil remains. Paleontologists literally "uncover" the history of ancient life on earth as they examine the fossils of long ago.

Geologist: A scientist who studies the history and features of the earth as recorded in its rocks. Geologists can decipher what might have happened on earth in the past, such as during the ice ages and the formation of mountains. They also help predict what might happen in the future (volcanic eruptions such as the one at Mount St. Helens in Washington State [USA] in 1980).

Zoologist: A scientist who studies the characteristics of animals other than humans. Zoologists classify animals into similar groups and help in the understanding of how animals evolved and what traits animals of the past might have had.

Botanist: A scientist who studies the characteristics and life cycles of plants. Botanists help us to understand the types of plants that grew in past times and how changes in ancient plant life might have affected the ancient animals and humans.

THE FAMILY ALBUM: A STEP TOWARD HUMANKIND

As the centuries passed, these humanlike creatures walked more and more upright. From the fossil record, we know, too, that their brains gradually increased in size. If you could take a look back through the family album, here are some of the relatives you might meet. (Look at the time line on page 90 to see how these relatives line up — all the way to you and your present-day family!)

THE AUSTRALOPITHECINES

It is not known what happened to the Lucy hominids. Perhaps they became extinct. Or, perhaps they simply evolved into *Australopithecus africanus* ("southern ape of Africa"), a larger-brained creature that followed *afarensis*. *Africanus* lived 2 to 3 million years ago.

Australopithecus robustus ("robust southern ape") came during and after *africanus*, living in southern Africa from 1.6 to 2.5 million years ago. This animal had huge teeth and jaws. Its jaw was so big, in fact, that it had to have a ridge (called a *sagittal crest*) atop its skull just to help hold up its massive chewing muscles! (This creature could easily chomp old frozen fruitcakes in half with a single bite!)

Some of the bones of *robustus* have been found near antelope horns. Scientists think the horns may have been used as digging tools.

Because members of *robustus* were slow runners and had few defenses, they were often eaten by the big predators of the day. Indeed, few *robustus* specimens survived beyond the age of 18. Their bones are often covered with bite marks from saber-toothed tigers and hyenas. One *robustus* child's skull was found with two deep holes in the top — the bite punctures of a leopard. Remarkably, the jaw and teeth fossils of a leopard were found in the same cave as the child's skull!

Who Had It Rougher?

Just how rough did prehistoric children have it? Why not spend a day living like one and find out for yourself?

➤ *Take a bath in cold water with no soap, no washcloth, no rubber ducky, and no towel.* Hominid kids didn't even have the tub. A dip in the river qualified as a bath.

➤ *Don't brush your teeth all day.* (Well, maybe you can just pretend on this one.) Since prehistoric people didn't eat sugar and candy, their teeth were remarkably free of cavities. Still, can you imagine playing next to a friend who never brushed her teeth? Ever? Eeeeeuw!

➤ *Don't use electricity.* Go the entire day without televisions, radios, computers, stoves, microwaves, toasters, refrigerators, telephones, lights, electric toys, and battery-run toys.

➤ *Go to the bathroom in the woods.* (Assuming you live near woods where nobody can see you!) Think about what else you could use besides toilet paper. (What do you think prehistoric kids used, Charmin?)

➤ *Don't run water in the house.* Take a jug of water outside and use it to drink and wash. Prehistoric kids would have used a nearby pond or stream.

➤ *Walk everywhere.* Prehistoric people didn't even ride the local animals.

➤ *For one day, eat only raw vegetables, fruits, and sunflower seeds.* Our ancestors ate everything uncooked for millions of years — even tough, old meat!

➤ *Sleep next to your siblings either on the floor (no beds!) or, if it's warm and you have permission, outside.* Prehistoric families very likely slept closely curled together for warmth and safety.

Behold! Nutcracker Man!

With a nickname like that, what do you suppose this hominid's most prominent feature was?

Living at the same time as *robustus,* but in another part of Africa (see map, page 61), was a hominid called *Australopithecus boisei* ("Boise's southern ape"). It was small-brained but more massive than *robustus* and had teeth twice as broad as postage stamps! No wonder it was given the nickname "nutcracker man."

Besides saber-toothed tigers, *robustus* and *boisei* lived among some rather scary neighbors.

An enormous early breed of sheep that stood 7 feet (2 m) tall and sported horns that would span the length of a midsized automobile today.

Tusked pigs as big as rhinoceroses. (Scientists who discovered their remains originally thought the tusks belonged to an elephant.)

Baboons as ferocious as today's, only twice as large.

Guess when Mom said, "No going out at night!" there was no argument. It was a rather dangerous neighborhood indeed!

Hunters & Warriors

From watching chimpanzees, we know that our earliest ancestors almost certainly hunted other animals for meat. Like chimps, they probably attacked in groups, screaming and throwing their arms about to confuse their prey. They most likely used rocks and clubs, as well as their bare hands, to take down their unlucky victims.

As intelligence developed, however, all manner of terrible weapons were created.

The hominids "fought" as hunters for their survival. Is that what our wars are about now? Do you think peace-loving peoples or warriors will be the ultimate survivors?

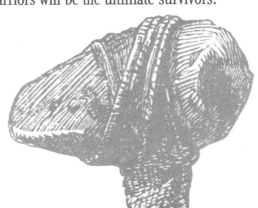

Speaking of Neighborhoods ...

No doubt about it, *robustus* and *boisei* lived in a tough part of town. And what about you? Would you characterize your neighborhood as friendly or hostile? Safe or dangerous? Calm or tense? Do you feel safe walking home after school? Would a neighbor help you if you had a problem?

It is a lot harder for kids to feel safe these days, but don't suffer in silence. Talk about how you feel with grown-ups and other kids, and see if you can put together a "safety network."

Check Out a Web Site!

❖ http://www.talkorigins.org/origins/
Answers your questions about evolution, with excellent links.

❖ http://www.nationalgeographic.com/outpost/index.html
Has an in-depth section on human origins, including photos, field studies, and links.

❖ http://www.indiana.edu/~origins
Human origins and evolution in Africa, with many links to museums.

To surf the Internet for other good sites, search under "human evolution" (use the quotation marks) and go to sites with an .edu ending — these indicate university and educational sites.

Speaking in Gestures

Our earliest ancestors could not "speak" as we do, but they probably communicated with grunts, growls, shouts, and gestures. Try getting through an entire day without speaking a single word. See if you can communicate with your friends and family. (To help you out, think about Koko, the famous gorilla that learned to speak with sign language.) Figure out a sign language, or pantomime, or make up gestures. If you were a hominid, could you communicate the important information below with gestures and grunts?

- I lost my spear.
- Baby sister is missing!
- Those berries are poisonous!
- A bad storm is coming.
- We will go hunting for mammoth at sunrise.
- Do you want to eat now?
- I'm very sick.
- I think I am going to have a baby!
- Og was eaten by a lion!
- The angry tiger is coming!

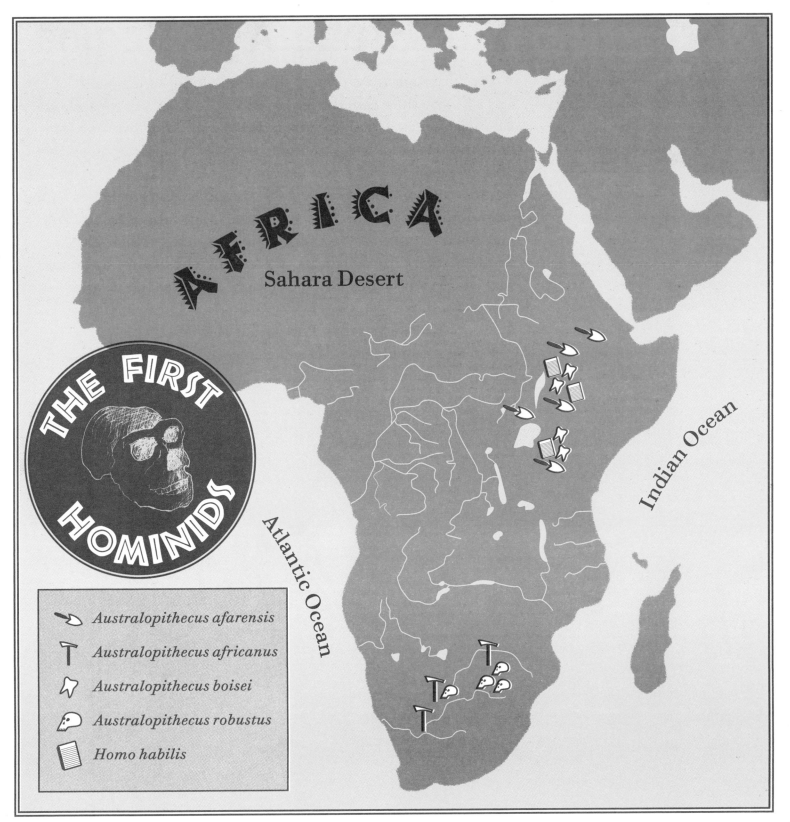

THE FIRST HOMINIDS

AFRICA

Sahara Desert

Atlantic Ocean

Indian Ocean

Australopithecus afarensis

Australopithecus africanus

Australopithecus boisei

Australopithecus robustus

Homo habilis

The Stone Age Begins

Although the "robust" hominids had the biggest brains yet, they weren't as big as those belonging to *Homo habilis*, which lived from 1.5 to 2 million years ago. This hominid was among the first to use stone tools. Thus, the name "Stone Age."

Indeed, their crude stone tools, along with their bones, are often found along lake and river shores throughout Africa. Animal remains found at *habilis* campsites suggest that they ate birds, catfish, frogs, lizards, mice, ostriches, pigs, rats, and snakes. They probably ate insects, nuts, berries, fruit, and bird eggs as well.

How could we possibly know what they ate?

Paleoanthropologists can sometimes guess what hominids ate simply by examining their teeth. Teeth that are smooth probably chewed a soft diet, comprised largely of fruit. Teeth that are chipped, scratched, and gouged probably chewed on seeds, gritty tubers, and bones.

A Common Need

Hominid fossils are almost always found near bodies of water. It's an interesting observation, and it tells us that like humans today, our earliest ancestors needed water to survive. Humans can stay alive for only 30 days or so without food, but only as long as *three* days without water!

Teeth Tales

Check out *your* teeth. What do they tell about what you eat? What might future beings think if they found humans with gold or silver fillings, or colorful braces and orthodontic headgear?

It's *Homo erectus!*

Homo erectus ("upright man") lived from 1.8 million to 27,000 years ago. (Why, that's just about yesterday in geological time!) This next-in-line hominid had an even bigger brain than *habilis*. (Notice how the brain's getting bigger and bigger with time? Evolution at work!)

With its ability to control fire (a major step forward), *erectus* was the first to migrate to colder climates, away from the African continent. Its fossils have been found throughout Europe and Asia, as well as Africa. In cold climates, *erectus* often spent winter months in caves, where it slept on animal pelts and maintained fires.

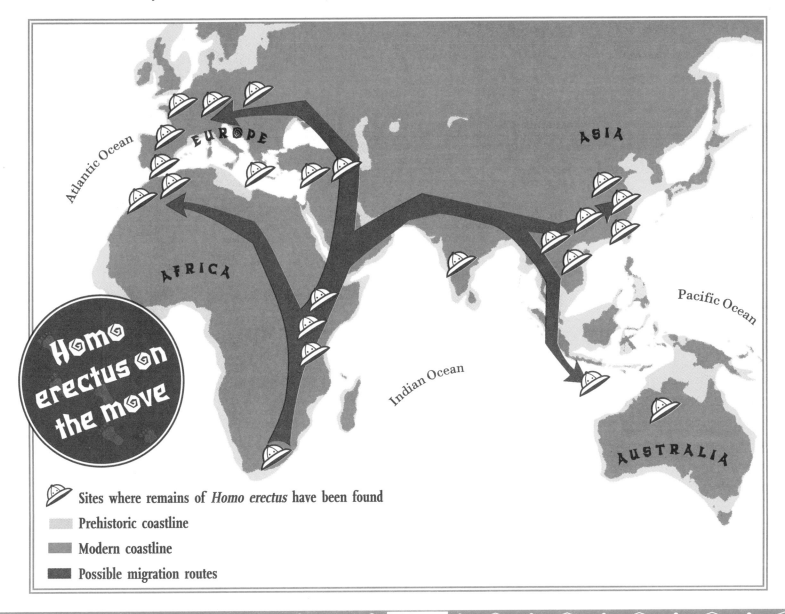

Homo erectus on the move

Atlantic Ocean

EUROPE

ASIA

AFRICA

Pacific Ocean

Indian Ocean

AUSTRALIA

Sites where remains of *Homo erectus* have been found

Prehistoric coastline

Modern coastline

Possible migration routes

Tools of the (Prehistoric) Trade

Homo erectus *greatly improved the toolmaking skills of her ancestors. The first hand ax, for example, originated with these hominids. So did spears. Recent finds prove that* erectus *made them at least 400,000 years ago. To get a sense of how simple and crude their tools were, see what you can make using only the materials described.*

Hand ax. *These weren't really used like the axes of today, but somehow we've named them that. Find a sharp rock and tie it to the end of a short, but heavy stick. You now know what the first hand ax looked like.*

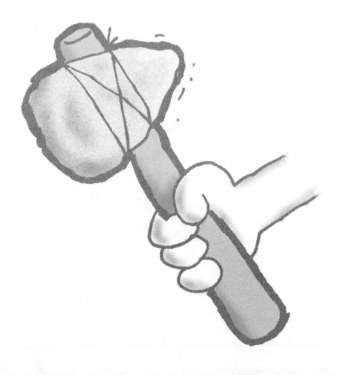

Spear. *Find a long stick and a sharp rock. Hone the tip of the stick with the rock until you have a point. Congratulations! You're a prehistoric spear-maker!*

Fire Up the Barbecue!

Scientists aren't certain when pre-humans first began using fire. Most certainly, hominids would have seen grass and forest fires from lightning strikes. The sight of flames sweeping over their homeland must have been terrifying, but there may have been a great benefit: "cooked" animals to eat!

It may be that early hominids simply "captured" these naturally caused fires and brought them home with them (in the form of smoldering tree branches, perhaps). It's unlikely that they knew how to actually start a fire, so great care must have been taken to keep these "found" fires from going out.

In time, they would learn about fire-starting methods like rubbing two sticks together. But we can guess that this was a very slow learning process.

OG, SPEAK UP!

Scientists know *erectus* used some sort of language, because his hunting skills were so much sharper than previous hominids. Hunting successfully in a group (without a gun) requires lots of careful communication. ("Og, get the heck out of that tiger's mouth, you numbskull!")

Judging by the bones of elephants, rhinos, giant boars, warthogs, and deer found buried in their campsites, *erectus* talked among themselves a lot!

Communication became, quite simply, vital for survival. The world was a much more unforgiving place then than we know it today. A broken leg or a bad infection almost certainly meant an early death — as did running into a lion or leopard. In northern climates, some members of *erectus* probably froze to death. These hominids had to share their knowledge to keep each other alive and healthy. ("By the way, Og, it's not a good idea to swallow a moose bone whole.")

THE FIRST CHATTERBOXES

Scientists can make a pretty good guess about when humans began speaking. The best clue they have is a hole. That's right, a *hole*. Not just any hole, but a hole in the skull.

You see, the tongue's movements are controlled by a nerve, the *hypoglossal* (hiy-po-GLOS-ul). To connect to the brain, the hypoglossal passes through a hole or "canal" in the skull. In early hominid skulls, such as Lucy, this hole is very small. That means the nerve was also very small.

But in later hominids, especially in those beginning about 500,000 years ago, the hole is much *larger*. That means the nerve controlling the tongue was much larger and likely more complex; therefore, it could probably have helped the tongue form complex sounds, such as words. Maybe even really difficult words. Lucy, on the other hand, could probably do little more than grunt. *Amazing what scientists can figure out from a tiny hole!*

hypoglossal canal

Bigfoot's Afoot!

Living in caves in China at about the same time as *erectus* (and dying out less than a million years ago) was a frightening ape-like beast called *Gigantopithecus*. From the remains of its massive jaws, scientists estimate this hominid stood as tall as 10 feet (3 m) and weighed as much as 1,200 pounds (540 kg)! Yes, a really big Bigfoot!

Now you'd imagine it would be hard to hide a creature this big, or at least that someone might be curious about its footprints! But the ancient existence of *Gigantopithecus* was discovered not through its footprints, but through its massive teeth (six times as wide as our own!).

Scientists are still searching sites in China in hopes of finding out more about this awesome and mysterious brute.

You and *Gigantopithecus*

Grab a piece of chalk and a tape measure. Ask an adult to go outside with you to either the side of your home or to a tall tree. Have the adult mark a spot 10 feet (3 m) up either on a wall or on the tree. This is how tall Gigantopithecus *stood. The adult you choose to help you will probably need a stepladder to reach that high! (Wonder if* Gigantopithecus *played basketball?)*

10 ft.

Think About It!

Bigfoot Today?

Every now and then, there is a report of a supposed modern-day sighting of Bigfoot. Where do you think these tales of sightings come from? Could they be based on truth? After all, a million years ago isn't that long in evolutionary terms. Could it be that Bigfoot isn't extinct? Or, is he simply alive and well in our imaginations?

Our Antecessor — Umm — Ancestor!

Although related, modern humans did not directly evolve from *erectus*. Paleoanthropologists believe modern humans arose from an African relative, *Homo antecessor* (ANT-uh-sess-or), which lived about 800,000 years ago.

Antecessor had an astonishingly modern face (scientists know this from the remains of an 11-year-old boy found in an ancient cave in Spain). It is known to have migrated to points throughout Europe, where it further evolved into a

being known as *heidelbergensis* (HI-dul-berg-EN-sis). *Heidelbergensis* had a large brain and was considerably ahead of those who came before. (But its canine teeth, according to one fossil find, were about twice the size of ours!)

Banned! The Evolution Controversy

In the 1920s, laws were passed that actually *banned* the teaching of evolution in some public schools. That is, students could not be told that humans and apes had common ancestors. People were afraid that if children knew about evolution, they might stop believing in the Bible — and in God.

"How can teachers tell students that they came from monkeys and not expect them to act like monkeys?" was the frequently repeated phrase of the time.

But a teacher in Tennessee thought children should be taught about the science of evolution. He thought the ban on evolution was wrong. In 1925, John Scopes boldly taught his class that plants, animals, and humans had developed and changed — sometimes dramatically — over millions of years. By teaching his students this lesson — a lesson about evolution — *Scopes had broken the laws* of the state of Tennessee.

Although many cheered his courage, others were outraged. They demanded that Scopes be punished for his crime, and he was quickly brought before a court of law. His court case, known as the "Scopes Monkey Trial" or "Scopes Evolution Trial," was argued by two of the nation's most brilliant law experts, Clarence Darrow and William Jennings Bryan. The entire trial, heard over radio from July 10 to July 21, 1925, was followed closely by people across the country.

After a tough battle, Scopes lost his case and was convicted for teaching evolution illegally. Religious leaders were jubilant. The victory eventually helped pave the way to making the teaching of evolution illegal in even more states.

For nearly 40 years after the famous trial, textbooks rarely dared mention evolution, even though science had clearly proved its existence. Schoolbook publishers were afraid that if they wrote about evolution, some schools might not buy their books.

Teacher John Scopes thought the ban on teaching evolution in schools was wrong.

For years, people have argued over which should be taught in schools. The Bible's creation story? Evolution? Or both?

In 1987 the matter was finally settled. The Supreme Court of the United States ruled that the Bible's version of creation was a "religious theory" and could not be taught as "science" in public schools. Scores of scientific organizations, science teacher associations, and *72 Nobel Prize winners in science* — among the most scholarly and brilliant people on earth — backed the decision and agreed it was right.

Today, public school teachers teach their students that humans evolved from ape-like ancestors. And parents are free to teach their children about the Bible's or their religious book's version of creation at home or in their place of worship.

Think About It!

Two of My Favorite Books

So, here's the thing. Say you have always loved hearing Bible stories or reading your religion's sacred book, and, say, science is your favorite subject. (You bring your science book home even when you don't have homework!)

What's the problem?

Nothing! No problem.

Your science book teaches you about facts and careful observations, and how to apply what we know to what we don't yet understand. Science helps us understand ourselves and our world, and it has improved life for millions of people. (Heard of any cases of bubonic plague lately?)

The Bible isn't a scientific textbook. It was never meant to be. It is a book about faith, and spirituality, and moral character. It, too, helps us understand ourselves and the people of the world, and it, too, has guided millions of people toward being better human beings and living better lives.

Most of us need science *and* faith in our lives to be good people who care for one another and for our earth.

GETTING CLOSER TO US!

Whew! We've been through a lot of evolution! But it can take a long time for one animal to change into another animal. Or for one animal to change into a human!

By now you may begin to see a pattern emerging: As larger brains evolved, our ancestors learned to do more. And the more they learned to do, the better they survived. By this time, the hominids were looking and acting much more like humans than like apes. They were also living longer.

THE NEANDERTHALS: ACTUAL HUMANS!

All of that continued as *Homo sapiens neanderthalensis* or Neanderthal (nee-AN-der-tall) man arrived on the scene about 200,000 years ago. The Neanderthals were named after the valley in western Germany, the Neander Thal, where their bones were first found in 1856. Their fossils have been found in and around caves in Germany, Spain, Italy, the Middle East, and elsewhere (see map). They are one of the most written about, yet most mysterious, of all the hominids.

Who were the famous Neanderthals? Examination of Neanderthal bones reveal that these beings walked for great distances with their children, foraging for food. These hominids were stockier and more muscular than today's humans. They were probably immensely strong. One expert believes a Neanderthal man living today could easily pick up the largest of our football players and hold him over its head — *and then hurl him over a goalpost!*

But their most interesting physical traits may have been the protruding ridges above their eyebrows, and their broad noses. Although the front of their skulls was rather flat and low, the rear of their heads sometimes had a distinct bulge, sometimes called an *occipital bun.* Their teeth were large by modern standards, as were their jaws.

Judging by the size of their skulls, Neanderthal brains were as large and sometimes even larger than our own. Still, they weren't as clever, apparently, as their brain size might indicate. They made shelters of animal skins and poles, some 60 different kind of tools, and even a few musical instruments. But most of the tools found in their campsites appear quite simple in design.

These hominids disappeared about 30,000 years ago.

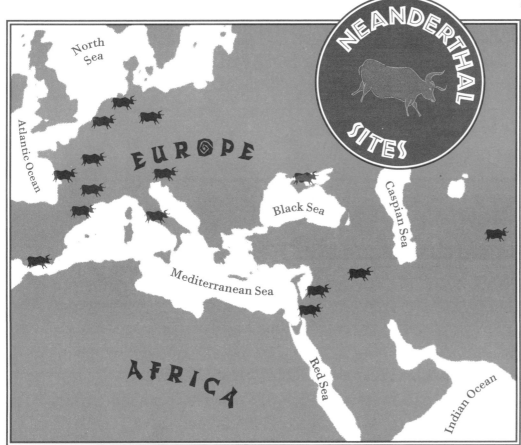

NEANDERTHAL SITES

CHECK YOUR POSTURE

Originally, Neanderthals were thought to have walked stooped over. It turns out that this is because the first skeleton discovered had arthritis and was badly deformed. From more than a hundred other complete skeletons that have been found — all free of arthritis — scientists now know that Neanderthals walked upright, just as we do.

Scientific Debate

The Neanderthals were among the first of the long line of hominids to be considered actual human beings. Therefore, they belong to the genus species, or class, known as *Homo sapiens*, or "wise man." (A lesser-known hominid called "archaic" *Homo sapiens* was actually the first creature to be considered fully human. Although its fossil record is sketchy, its remains are Neanderthal-like in many ways.)

But there is still some disagreement about whether Neanderthals belong to the class of *Homo sapiens*, the class that we belong to. Some scientists are arguing that the Neanderthals might be a separate species, completely unrelated to humans. Others believe they mated with other hominids at the time, eventually giving birth to the first fully modern humans.

Think About It!

Discussion versus Argument

Do you know the difference between an argument and a discussion or informal debate? Do you ever feel as if you are being attacked when you are expressing your views? Well, being attacked is not part of a discussion. First and foremost in a discussion is that all viewpoints are treated with respect.

Scientific debate is good because it raises the questions that fuel the search for more factual evidence. In science, finding evidence to support a *hypothesis* is the number-one goal. All debate is good because it expands our thinking and leads us to look more deeply into a subject, bringing us closer to the truth.

In the art of real debate, such as the members of a debating team practice, a person should be able to defend either point of view — even the one he or she doesn't personally believe in!

Only in the Movies!

Neanderthals are usually portrayed brutishly in Hollywood's "cave man" movies, with lots of club-swinging and grunting but little actual talking. (Experts think Neanderthals probably spoke, but not very well.)

Many movies depicting our ancient human ancestors are laughably inaccurate. The biggest error these movies make is pitting dinosaurs against cave men (see page 44), a situation that could never have happened in real life. Check out *One Million Years B.C.* (1967), starring Raquel Welch, for big yucks. Count how many things you find wrong in this movie!

Planet of the Apes (1968) is a fantastic story about reverse evolution and is considered a classic. (Apes who evolved from humans instead of the other way around.)

A great documentary that's true to life (as we know it) is *Mysteries of Mankind*, produced by the National Geographic Society.

A fabulous movie based on the famous Scopes Evolution Trial (see page 68) is *Inherit the Wind* (1960), with Spencer Tracy. The writing and acting are superb, and the story asks some truly profound questions.

fresh

Pop Corn

WHO'S AROUND?

Roughly 30,000 years ago, there was not one, not two, but *three* different types of humans in the world. These were *Homo erectus*, the Neanderthals, and the Cro-Magnons.

I'm with Neanderthal

I'm with Cro-Magnon

I'm with them

A NEANDERTHAL BURIAL

In August 1993, scientists examining a cave near the Syrian city of Aleppo unearthed a 5-foot (1.5-m) pit dug 50,000 to 70,000 years ago. At the bottom of the pit lay the skeleton of a 2-year-old Neanderthal child who was lying on its back with knees up and arms extended. A triangular shard of flint — perhaps a blade of some sort — rested over its heart.

Anthropologists knew the child could be no older than 2 because of the number of teeth in its mouth. When they measured the tot's braincase (skull), however, they were astonished to find it to be the same size as that of a modern 6-year-old's! That means the toddler had a huge brain for its age. But this is not unusual. Many Neanderthals apparently had larger brains than our own.

A Neanderthal flint.

The Greatest Fossil Hunters of All Time

The honor for the greatest human fossil hunters of the 20th century must go to the Leakey family, Louis, Mary, and Richard, who dedicated their lives to discovering the story of human evolution. Since 1931, this family of paleoanthropologists and their team of explorers have been responsible for unearthing specimens from *Homo habilis*, *Homo erectus*, the famous footprints at Tanzania, and scores of other important fossils that, among other things, proved that humans evolved in Africa. Louis died in 1972, and Mary made many contributions to the field until she died in 1996. Richard partially lost both of his legs in a 1993 plane crash but is still active as the head of the Kenya Wildlife Service, and his wife and daughter continue the Leakey tradition. They currently are leading teams for new searches for human fossils in Africa today. You can read about the Leakeys' work in the book, *Origins Reconsidered*, by Richard Leakey.

The Cro-Magnons: A Big Step Forward

Skull of a 17- to 18-year-old Cro-Magnon girl, found at a Stone Age site in Les Eyzies, France.

Fully modern or nearly fully modern-appearing humans existed at least 100,000 years ago. These people lived side by side with the Neanderthals for centuries. They may have mated with Neanderthals. We may never know for sure.

One thing we *do* know is that modern *Homo sapiens* were considerably smarter than the Neanderthals. Among these modern humans were the Cro-Magnons (cro-MAN-yuns), the white ancestors of modern Europeans. Cro-Magnons are named after the cave in southwest France where their remains were first discovered. They lived from about 40,000 to 10,000 years ago.

Except for a slightly broader face and lower forehead, Cro-Magnons were almost exactly like us. In fact, if you were to pass one on the street, you wouldn't look twice.

Cro-Magnons invented the bow and arrow, the spear thrower, the harpoon, the fish hook, the fish net, the fueled lamp, the first primitive calendar, the sewing needle, tailored leggings and tunics, collared shirts and cuffed sleeves, and art. Very impressive!

Unlike the Neanderthals before them, they painted their faces and bodies, wore jewelry, and buried their dead with elaborate funeral rituals.

Build a Miniature Found-Material Shelter

Cro-Magnons built a wide variety of shelters of wood, stone, bone (mammoth bones were sometimes used for framing), and animal skins. In some parts of the world, they killed giant armadillos, stripped them of their automobile-sized shells, and used them for temporary houses. An amazingly clever use of available materials!

Stake out a small area in your kitchen. This is where you live, Cro-Magnon-style! Now, see if you are as clever at using found materials to create a good shelter as the Cro-Magnons were at using armadillo shells.

Anything goes (with grown-up approval, of course) as long as it would keep you dry, warm, and protected from dangerous animals and violent storms. What will it be — marshmallow walls supporting a sandwich-bag-foil roof, or are you considering using some goopy flour-water paste for a toothpick structure? Are you as clever as those Cro-Magnons in their cozy armadillo-shell homes?

VILLAGE OF BONES

Scientists in the Ukraine in 1975 began studying the remains of a 15,000-year-old village made entirely of mammoth bones. The homes and buildings, measuring 12 to 21 feet (4 to 7 m) across, were constructed from the bones of a whopping 149 woolly mammoths! Half of one home was made from a stack of jawbones and skulls. Now, is that eerie or what?

Love & Compassion

THE EVOLUTION SOLUTION

CARE FOR THE ELDERLY

Although the maximum life span for a Neanderthal was 45, Cro-Magnons lived much longer, often to 60 or 65. Older hominids had a higher chance of dying from disease or injury, but there was great value in keeping them alive. What do you think are some good reasons (besides loving them) for keeping the older hominids from dying too soon?

Among the most wonderful developments in evolving humankind were feelings. Even animals have powerful feelings for their young — so powerful that they will risk their own lives for them in times of danger. (Mother bears are most dangerous and most likely to attack you when they have their cubs with them.)

In hominids and then in *Homo sapiens*, a growing ability to feel for others undoubtedly aided the survival of the species. Consider this: If someone loves you enough to carry you around after you've broken your ankle, you'll not only return the favor, but you will live and then perhaps go on to mate with other humans and have children. Yet, without that critical help, you may have been left to die.

Neanderthals took care of their sick and injured, but the Cro-Magnons did so even more. They were clearly a compassionate people.

SMACK!

ARTISTS, TOO!

Look at the background art on this book's cover. It shows a famous cave painting at the Lascaux Cave in Dordogne, France, from about 15,000 years ago. It was the Cro-Magnons who drew and painted the beautiful pictures of animals in caves throughout Europe. These paintings can still be seen today, thousands of years after they were made!

Re-create Ancient Art!

Prehistoric people produced a variety of artworks, from cave paintings of animals and hunting scenes, to outdoor rock engravings, to various figurines and body ornaments. One prehistoric skeleton of a 12-year-old boy was found wearing a belt made of 240 fox teeth! You can make some of these artworks yourself from simple tools.

Handprints on rock. *Australian aborigines (believed to be the original people on the Australian continent) made these on rock faces as long as 50,000 years ago.*

Paint some red or white fingerpaints on your hand and press onto a large, flat rock. Get your whole family to do this on one large rock or several small ones — sort of a family nameplate!

Chiseled rock engravings, or petroglyphs. *Using a black crayon, draw the outline of a prehistoric mammal (mammoth, rhino, saber-toothed tiger, giant ground sloth) on the softest, flattest-faced rock you can find. Using another sharper rock, scratch the animal's outline into the colored outline. (Some rocks will scratch out chalky lines; these are the best kinds of rocks to use.) Leave your engraving outside for archaeologists to find far in the future. Some engravings can last hundreds of thousands of years!*

Clay creations. *Shape a large piece of clay into prehistoric animals, artistic pendants, and beads for stringing. (Ancient humans spent thousands of hours making and stringing beads to wear.) More than one prehistoric artist used mammoth tusks to carve figures and designs on. You can do much the same by molding a large piece of clay into the shape of a tusk. Then, score and engrave a design (our ancestors liked to engrave hoof marks of animals) with a pencil, stick, or other small object.*

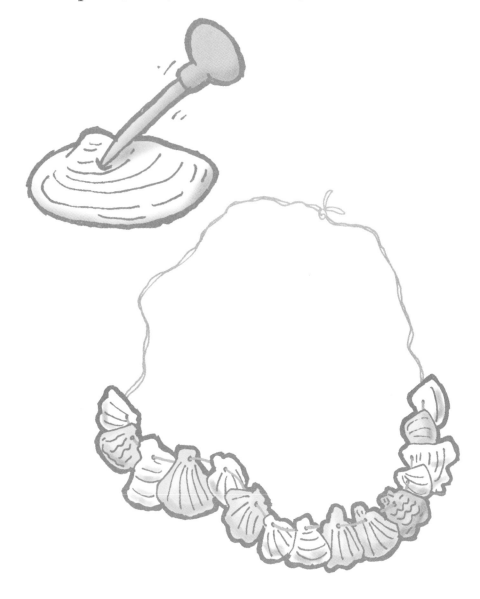

Make a shell necklace. *Cro-Magnons spent time making ornaments of seashells. If you live near the ocean, gather a handful of old scallop shells and clamshells. Pierce them with an awl or nail (ask an adult to help you as the shells are very brittle and sharp). String them together to make a necklace or anklet. Don't live near a beach? Fashion shells out of clay instead.*

WE'RE HERE! MODERN HUMANS & OUR EVOLVING FUTURE

Human beings are thought to have arrived in North or South America from Asia as long as 15,000 to 30,000 years ago. (Scientists know for sure people were here at least 13,000 years ago. They may have come either by boat or by a land bridge that is now covered by water.) These Asians would later be known as Indians and Native Americans.

A few thousand years later, the Cro-Magnons of Europe either vanished or blended into the growing population of fully modern humans, the *Homo sapiens sapiens*.

LOOK FOR THE EVIDENCE

How do we know that humans evolved in Africa and not somewhere else, like America? The oldest fossils of humans and their ancestors have all been found in Africa; the second-oldest have all been found in Europe and Asia; later finds have been made in North and South America. Remains of *Homo sapiens sapiens* found in America have never been more than a few thousand years old, while those found in Africa may be millions of years old. It's amazing what ancient fossils can still tell us today!

A SENSE OF COMMUNITY

Humans soon began to congregate in towns, then cities. Eleven thousand years ago, the largest city on earth, Chemi Shanidar in Iraq, was populated with only 150 people.

Fifteen thousand years ago, sheep had little wool, chickens laid eggs only seasonally, and wild cows produced milk only when nursing young. But humans domesticated these animals and quickly learned how to breed them and increase their yields.

A short time later, the inventions of the *microlith* (cutting tool) and grinding stone made it possible to harvest and process large tracts of wild grain. All over the world humans began to give up the hunting and gathering way of life to take up this more secure way of *farming*. Domesticating animals and farming encouraged the development of community, because there was no longer a need to live nomadic lives in search of food.

Too Many People?

Today, the area around New York City is home for some 20 million *Homo sapiens sapiens.* Each year the world population of humans grows by more than 90 million! We now measure our worldwide population in billions, not millions.

True, we no longer have to worry about leopard attacks. Or dying from a broken leg. We have invented thousands of medicines to keep us well, and we have even learned how to transplant donated organs and rebuild joints that are worn out.

Most human beings now live well into their 80s. Many survive into their 100s. And we are happy about that!

But could there ever be so many *Homo sapiens sapiens* that we run out of the necessary food, air, water, and land for all of us to survive? Do you think the development of our brains throughout evolution will enable us to stay ahead of the growth of our population by learning such things as how to make salt-water from the ocean drinkable? Or might we evolve into creatures who eat less, use fewer natural resources, and maybe even breathe less oxygen?

Survival of the Fittest

Remember Charles Darwin (see page 35) and his observation of how those species that were best suited to survive in their environment would continue on? Well, it helps to explain a lot about how modern humans (that's all of us) are all related, but also have many differences.

For example, today scientists recognize three main races of humans: The Caucasoids (whites) make up 55 percent of the world's population; the Mongoloids (Asian), 33 percent; the Negroids (blacks), 8 percent.

Although we are indeed different on the surface, *all humans originated in Africa and once had dark skin.* The question is, why did the races go on to develop different skin colors?

Look to the Sun

The sun shines around the middle of the earth — the equator — more brightly than in northern or southern regions.

People who evolved near the equator, then, needed much more protection against sunburn and skin diseases caused by the sun's strong rays. That's why, in general, the closer you move toward the equator, the more dark-skinned people there are.

Dark skin protects against the sun's harmful rays much better than light skin. (Why, then, aren't South American people near the equator as dark as Africans? Because people arrived in South America only a few thousand years ago. They haven't had enough time to evolve darker skin as the Africans have.)

Less skin pigment, or color, is needed the farther north one lives. It is not simply that protection from the sun is less necessary, but also skin tones aid in the regulation of vitamin D formation, the main source of which is sunlight. Too much vitamin D causes kidney disease; not enough causes rickets.

So our varying skin tones enable the darker-skinned people to be protected from vitamin D–caused kidney disease and the lighter-skinned people to be protected from too little vitamin D and rickets.

In environments between the two extremes, humans evolved a light brown or yellowish skin. Eskimos, for example, have a yellowish tinge to help regulate their exposure to sunlight from the glare off the snow in snowy regions.

It's all quite amazing when you think about it — and it all makes perfect sense!

EQUATOR

A QUESTION OF BODY FAT

Did you know that some humans tend to grow more body fat than others? And it has nothing to do with good nutrition and skipping the junk food. Nothing at all.

It's evolution at work again — evolution that changed our bodies to protect us from the dangers of a hostile environment.

Once again we consider the sun, specifically the sun's heat or lack of it.

Humans, on average, have far less body fat in hot, equatorial regions of the world, and much more in cold regions. Why? *Fat is an excellent insulator against cold.*

That's why Eskimos tend to develop more body fat than any other people. The average Eskimo weighs 170 pounds (85 kg). By contrast, the average Irish person, who evolved in a warmer climate, weighs just 157 pounds (78 kg). At the far end of the scale, meanwhile, is the Algerian Berber, who evolved in intense desert heat and typically weighs in at just 125 pounds (62.5 kg)!

Every additional pound of fat creates an extra 200 miles (320 km) of blood vessels throughout the body! With more blood vessels, more blood can be pumped to warm a person's cold skin. Thus, Eskimos can tolerate freezing temperatures much better than anyone else.

Yes, body fat is an amazing adaptation that saved our fellow *Homo sapiens sapiens* in varying climates!

A Trick Question

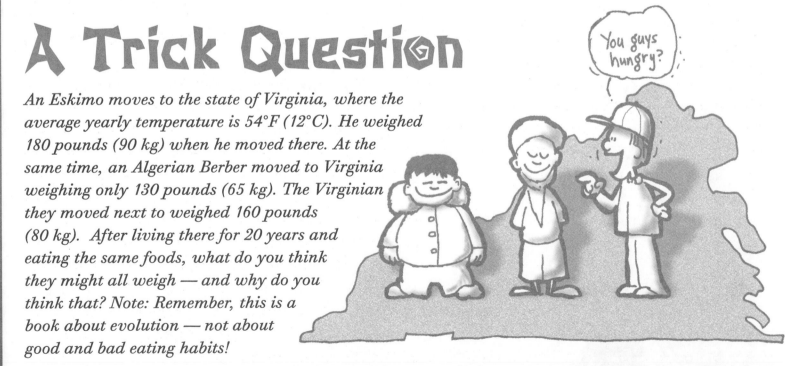

An Eskimo moves to the state of Virginia, where the average yearly temperature is 54°F (12°C). He weighed 180 pounds (90 kg) when he moved there. At the same time, an Algerian Berber moved to Virginia weighing only 130 pounds (65 kg). The Virginian they moved next to weighed 160 pounds (80 kg). After living there for 20 years and eating the same foods, what do you think they might all weigh — and why do you think that? Note: Remember, this is a book about evolution — not about good and bad eating habits!

You guys hungry?

Answer: They would all weigh about the same as when they arrived in Virginia, if they were leading a healthy lifestyle. Evolutionary changes — such as the amount of body fat in different human body types — takes a long time to change.

Why Are We the Size We Are?

Evolution seems to have experimented with the size of animals.

Size is sensitive to changes in the environment. One size may not fit all, at all times. That's why nature tends to develop a mixture of sizes in any animal group (lots of different-sized people, for example).

Although big animals can fight off smaller animals, smaller animals need less food and may be able to hold out longer in times of famine.

Animals stranded on islands tend to evolve down in size because food supplies are less abundant. They can't easily move to a new grazing area. Mammoth skeletons found on islands are often half the size of their counterparts on mainlands.

The tallest humans, on average, are the Dutch, with males growing to an average size of 5 feet 10 inches (1.75 m). The shortest are the pygmies, who stop growing at the age of 10 due to a lack of growth hormone. Pygmy males average only 4 feet 6 inches (1.25 m). Some variations in height are due to genes and are out of our control. But some can be traced to nutrition. Good diets have been shown to produce the largest humans, while poor diets, the smallest.

Might all humans one day be as small as pygmies? Can you think of any changes in the environment that could bring this about?

OUR FUTURE EVOLUTION

What surprises may evolution have in store for such a successful species in the future? Will we continue to evolve? Will humans develop even bigger brains? (If so, babies would have to be born with cone-shaped heads to emerge from the birth canal. But perhaps in time, women will evolve larger birth tracts.)

➤ Over the past 5 million years, our jaws have grown progressively smaller. *Will our jaws continue to shrink?* Will our teeth? Will we develop fewer teeth?

➤ *How might the human nose and lungs change* if we continue to breathe polluted air? Could we one day adapt to breathe dirty air and still be healthy?

➤ *How might the earth's vanishing ozone layer affect human evolution?* With more of the sun's damaging rays shining through, will nature favor dark-skinned humans over light ones?

➤ *What if our population continues to grow?* In an overcrowded world with vanishing resources, would nature favor the development of smaller humans? If so, how small? Might we one day stand only 18 inches (45 cm) tall? (And be called *Homo sapiens munchkinius?*)

Think About It!

Will Our Beasts Get Us?

It seems that evolution has taken care of everything — varied skin tones to protect us from the sun, varying levels of fat to protect us from the cold, and even varying sizes. We have highly evolved brains with which to solve problems presented by disease. We should, in fact, be equipped to deal with just about everything.

So, what's one of our biggest problems then? *The human race.* That's right, we are our own worst enemy! We can't seem to get along with one another. We have wars over different religions. We have made our streets and neighborhoods unsafe because different races don't accept one another.

We are all one and the same. Those of different color have each evolved to survive their environments. What are *you* going to do to get this message across to your family, friends, classmates, and neighbors — and your government? *What are you going to do to save the human race?*

Time Travel!

There you are. Well, not really you, but your descendants one million years from now. Oh, I know you don't quite recognize them. There were changes that had to be made to survive the … what? The bomb? The lack of water? No growing space? Our new settlement on a new planet? Who knows the cause.

Exactly what changes has evolution made for survival? Carve a figure of the future you from a bath-sized bar of soap, using a blunt butter knife. Or, sketch in pastels your vision of what you look like. Or, write an essay about a day in your "new" life. And ask yourself, have we improved? Have we learned anything? Or did we simply have to change to survive?

Fast-Forward on Evolution

Are humans speeding up the process of evolution?

We humans now travel all over the world (500 million international flights per year). As a result, we are unintentionally importing and exporting exotic germs, plants, and animals into places they were not meant to be. They are picked up on shoes, in ship's bilge water, and on fruits and vegetables.

It's a speeded-up form of evolution called *bioinvasion*, the quick transference of a living creature into a new and faraway environment. Sometimes these creatures die off instantly in their new environment. But sometimes they completely take over or destroy the new environment, endangering the plants and animals that already live there. And human beings are to blame.

- The Florida Everglades are literally being taken over by the exotic Australian melaleuca tree that is crowding out native plant species.

- The beautiful but prolific purple loosestrife is choking out native plants in New England.

- New England has exported the organism known as the comb jelly and ruined the anchovy fisheries in the Black Sea.

- Asian clams introduced to San Francisco Bay have destroyed phytoplankton, which many creatures there depend on for food.

- The Asian tiger mosquito is spreading throughout the world, bringing with it dengue fever and other diseases.

Humans meddling with nature may open a Pandora's box of unforeseen problems, especially when it comes to bioinvasion.

A Case in Point

In Micronesia, monitor lizards were imported to control sugar plantation rats.

But the lizards had a stronger taste for the area's poultry stocks, and so humans brought in poisonous toads to bring down the lizard population.

The lizards were killed off by the toads, but that led to a proliferation of beetles (that the lizards had eaten), which then infested and destroyed coconut trees.

At the same time, the cats, dogs, and pigs who tried to eat the toads also died, and because they did, the rat population was left free to grow to gigantic proportions!

Is there a lesson here?

Looking Ahead

So many questions. So much to think about. Scientists like to speculate about what lies ahead, but nobody can ever really know for certain.

For now the future of evolution is only something we can imagine.

What would Lucy have thought of us 3.2 million years ago?

Think about 3.2 million years from *today*. How strange will we look to the human of the future?

Will the new human look back and think that *we* looked like beasts?

What will this new human call itself, *Homo sapiens sapiens sapiens?*

Or will it even call itself human at all?

Homo sapiens sapiens have explored the deepest oceans. We have landed on the moon. We have sent probes to other worlds.

We have come a long way since Lucy. We are truly a successful species. Perhaps we are the most successful species nature ever produced.

But for how long?

From Ape People to Humans:

Ardipithecus ramidus
4.4 million years

➤ Remains found in the village of Aramis in Ethiopia, just 45 miles (72 km) from where the famous Lucy fossils were discovered. Parts of 17 different skeletons found; small and had skulls very much like Lucy. Elbows probably could not support knuckle walking, so *ramidus* must have walked upright part of the time. (Sign of intelligence, as knuckle walking is painful!) Lived in wooded environment.

Australopithecus anamensis
3.9 to 4.2 million years

➤ Discovered in South Africa in 1995. Shin bone is thicker than that of a chimpanzee, evidence of upright walking.

Australopithecus afarensis
3 to 4 million years

➤ Most famous fossils are Lucy, who stood only $3^1/_2$ feet (1 m) tall, and the footprint trail found in Tanzania.

Australopithecus africanus
2 to 3 million years

➤ Had a slightly larger brain than Lucy's.

Australopithecus robustus
1.6 to 2.5 million years

➤ Had huge teeth; jaw so heavy it required a special crest atop the skull to hold its muscles. Thought to have used antelope horns as digging tools. Evidence shows it was eaten often by predators.

Australopithecus boisei
1.6 to 2.5 million years

➤ Lived in another part of Africa at the same time as *robustus*. Was more massive than *robustus*, with extremely broad teeth.

Homo rudolfensis
1.9 to 2.5 million years

➤ From the Rift Valley in Africa. May have developed simple tools, such as stones for battering and flakes for cutting.

Homo habilis
1.5 to 2 million years

➤ Known as "handy man" because it made crude stone tools; thus period called the Stone Age. May have been first to migrate to Asia, along with *ergaster*.

An Annotated Time Line

Homo ergaster
1.4 to 2 million years

From the Rift Valley, along with *habilis* and also associated with simple stone tools. Was larger than *habilis*. Burned balls and patches of clay found in their campsites suggest they used fire. May have been the first to migrate to Asia.

Homo erectus
27,000 to 1.8 million years

Fittingly named "upright man." Inner ear structure, where the body's sense of balance is centered, appears more humanlike than any earlier hominid. That means it walked and ran exactly like us. Remains found in Africa, China, and Europe. It or a very close relative may have been the first to arrive in Europe about 1 million years ago. Incredibly, an isolated late version survived on Java up until the time Cro-Magnons were in Europe, according to new estimates provided in 1996.

Homo antecessor
800,000 years

Strikingly modern-looking, according to fossil skeleton of an 11-year-old.

Homo heidelbergensis
200,000 to 500,000 years

Large-faced with massive brow ridges and a very low forehead. Remains found in Africa, China, and Europe.

"Archaic" Homo sapiens
250,000 years

The first modern human subspecies. Broad face, somewhat Neanderthal-like.

Homo sapiens neanderthalensis
30,000 to 230,000 years

Neanderthal man. Stocky and strong with brains sometimes larger than fully modern humans (but not particularly intelligent). Back of its skull bulged out to form a curious "bun."

Homo sapiens (Cro-Magnon man)
10,000 to 40,000 years

Had a slightly broader face than fully modern humans, but if you saw one on a bus today, you wouldn't look twice. Highly intelligent and advanced.

Homo sapiens sapiens
The Present

"Double wise man." All humans who are alive today. (Well, okay, almost all.)

MUSEUMS TO VISIT

Learn more about our ancestors and evolution at these museums (and check out the Web sites on page 59).

UNITED STATES AND CANADA

The Academy of Natural Sciences, Philadelphia, PA (*phone* 215/299-1060)

American Museum of Natural History, New York, NY (*phone* 212/769-5100; *Web site* http://www.amnh.org/)

Bishop Museum, Honolulu, HI (*phone* 808/847-8256)

Carnegie Museum of Natural History, Pittsburgh, PA (*phone* 412/622-1975; *Web site* http://www.clpgh.org/cmnh/)

Cleveland Museum of Natural History, Cleveland, OH (*phone* 216/231-4600)

The Exploratorium, San Francisco, CA (*phone* 415/563-7337; *Web site* http://www.exploratorium.edu/)

Fernbank Museum of Natural History, Atlanta, GA (*phone* 404/370-8077; *Web site* http://www.fernbank.edu/museum/)

The Field Museum of Natural History, Chicago, IL (*phone* 1-800-FIELD-54)

Museum of Science, Boston, MA (*phone* 800/344-0432)

National Museum of Natural History, Smithsonian Institution, Washington, DC (*phone* 202/357-2700; *Web site* http://www.mnh.si.edu/)

Natural History Museum of Los Angeles County, Los Angeles, CA (*phone* 213/763-DINO; *Web site* http://www.nhm.org/)

Provincial Museum of Alberta, Edmonton, AB, Canada (*Web site* http://www.pma.edmonton.ab.ca/)

Royal British Columbia Museum, Victoria, BC, Canada (*Web site* http://rbcm1.rbcm.gov.bc.ca/)

Royal Ontario Museum, Toronto, ON, Canada (*Web site* http://www.rom.on.ca)

San Diego Natural History Museum, San Diego, CA (*phone* 619/232-3821; *Web site* http://www.sdnhm.org/)

WORLD

Deutsches Museum, Munchen, Germany (reproduction of prehistoric cave and cave art)

Neandertal Museum, Talstrasse 300, D-40822 Mettmann, Germany (State-of-the-art re-creations of Neanderthal people and other prehumans)

le Prehistorama, Musée des Origines de l'Homme, Rousson, France

Musée National d'Histoire, Luxembourg

Natural History Museum, Berne, Switzerland

The Natural History Museum, London, England (*Web site* http://nhm.ac.uk/)

The Science Museum, London, England

Hunterian Museum, Glasgow, Scotland (*Web site* http://info.gla.ac.uk/Museum/guided/Hominid/)

The Museum of Natural History of the University of Pisa, Italy

BIBLIOGRAPHY

BOOKS

Darwin, Charles. *The Descent of Man.*

Dennett, Daniel. *Darwin's Dangerous Idea.* Simon and Schuster, 1995.

Lambert, David. *The Field Guide to Early Man.* Facts on File, 1987.

Life Before Man. Thames and Hudson, 1995.

McCutcheon, Marc. *The Compass in Your Nose & Other Fascinating Facts About Humans.* Tarcher/Putnams, 1989.

Roberts, J.M. *Prehistory and the First Civilizations.* Vol. 1 of *The Illustrated History of the World.* Oxford University Press, 1999.

Sattler, Helen. *Hominids.* Lothrop, Lee and Shepard, 1988.

Shreeve, James. *The Neanderthal Enigma.* James William Morrow, 1995.

Tattersall, Ian. *The Fossil Trail.* Oxford University Press, 1995.

Tattersall, Ian. *The Human Odyssey.* Prentice Hall, 1993.

Teaching About Evolution and the Nature of Science. National Academy of Sciences Press, 1998.

Tudge, Colin. *The Time Before History.* Touchstone, 1997.

JOURNALS

Archaeology (November/December 1995). "Earliest Bipedal Ancestor?"

Archaeology (January/February 1996). "The First Europeans" p. 36; "Treasure of the Sierra Atapuerca" p. 45; "Neanderthals of the Levant" p. 49.

Discover (January 1996). "Little Foot, Big Implications: Walking at Turkana" p. 66, 68.

Discover (December 1997). "The Face of an Ancestral Child" p. 88–101.

Discover (November 1998). "The Gift of Gab" p. 62; "Last Days of the Wonder Drugs" p. 78.

National Geographic (March 1996). "Face-to-Face with Lucy's Family" p. 96–117.

Natural History (May 1993). "The Dawn of Adornment" p. 61.

Natural History (September 1994). "Lucy on the Earth in Stasis" p. 12.

Natural History (March 1997). "Evolution and the Catholic Church" p. 16.

Science News (January 4, 1997). "Ancient Roads to Europe" p. 12–13.

Science News (December 1996). "*Homo erectus* Shows Staying Power in Java."

Science News (April 9, 1994). "Hominids: Down to Earth or Up a Tree?" p. 231.

Science News (October 1, 1994). "Team Unearths Oldest Known Human Ancestor" p. 212–13.

Science News (July 29, 1995). "Hominid Bones Show Strides Toward Walking" p. 71.

Science News (October 21, 1995). "Child's Bones Found in Neandertal Burial" p. 261.

Scientific American (April 1993). "Modern Humans in the Levant" p. 95.

Scientific American (April 1996). "Out of Food?" p. 20.

Time (August 28, 1995). "On Its Own Two Feet" p. 58.

Time (July 6, 1998). "Dinosaurs of a Feather" p. 82.

INDEX

A

activities
clay claws, making, 12
core samples, taking a
backyard, 46–47
debating, 72
extinction examples, 36
family traits, tracing, 26
fight-or-flight response, testing
your, 15
footprint casts, making,
52–53
found-material shelter,
building a, 76
generations comparison,
you and fruit fly, 29
Gigantopithecus,
measuring, 67
handprints on rocks,
making, 78
Hare Hide-and-Seek,
camouflage experiment, 25
keeping your "cool,"
animal anger, 18
knuckle walking, 51
measuring Lucy, 48
multi-generational
photograph, taking a, 29
one-armed survival, try
out, 38
petroglyph, chiseling, 78
prehistoric living, spend
a day, 57
prehistoric tools, make
your own, 64
scary storytelling, 14
shell necklaces,
making, 79
sleep survey, do a, 20
speaking in gestures, 60
Spot the Animal, play a
game, 6–7, 9–11, 13, 15–17
time travel to future, 87
weighing in, trick question, 84
whale evolution art, 31
See also Think About It!
adaptation, 22, 24–28, 35
Africa, 44, 48, 50–51, 58,
61–63, 74, 81, 90–91
America, North and South,
80, 81
anger, 17–18
anteaters, 34
anthropologists, 54
antiobiotics, 27–28
apes, 16, 21, 39–41, 51, 59, 60
appendixes, 11
Archaeopteryx, 32
Ardipithecus ramidus, 90
"archaic" *Homo sapiens*,
72, 91
art, 77–79
Asia, 63, 67, 71, 80, 81, 91
asteroid collision, 36
Australian aborigines, 78
Australopithecus afarensis
(Lucy), 44, 48–51, 61,
66, 90
skeleton of, 49
Australopithecus africanus,
56, 61, 90
Australopithecus anamensis,
90
Australopithecus boisei, 58,
61, 90
Australopithecus robustus,
56, 61, 90

B

baboons, 9, 58
beastly traits. *See* vestiges
Bible, 68–69
Bigfoot, 66–67
bioinvasion, 88
birds, 8, 32–33, 34
body language, 9–10, 13, 40, 60
body weight, 84–85
books, 10, 35, 74, 93
botanists, 54
brain
hominid, 40–42, 49, 55–56, 58,
62–63, 90
human, 33, 41, 71, 74, 91
brawn, 42
Bryan, William Jennings, 68
burials, 74–75

C

camouflage, 24–26
canine teeth. *See* teeth
Caudipteryx, 32
Chemi Shanidar, 81
chimpanzees, 40–41, 51, 59
China, 63, 66, 91
claws, 11–12
communication
nonverbal, 9–10, 13, 40, 60
verbal, 65–66, 73
communities, 81
compassion, 77
core samples, 46–47
creationism, 68–69
Cro-Magnons, 73, 75–77, 80, 91

D

Darrow, Clarence, 68
Darwin, Charles, 35, 82
Darwin, Erasmus, 35
debate, 72
defenses, animal, 9, 11, 13,
15, 24–26
Descent of Man, The (C.
Darwin), 35
dinosaurs, 32–33, 36, 44, 73
dogs, 7, 10, 13, 23

E

ears, 11
elderly, 77
elephants, 22, 32, 37
emotions, 17–18, 77
erector pili, 13
Eskimos, 83–84
Europe, 63, 67, 70–71, 75,
81, 91
evolution
about, 21–24, 26–31,
28, 35
controversy over, 35,
68–69
Evolution Solution, 11,
17, 26, 33, 72, 77, 81
in the future, 82, 86–89
of human beings. *See*
hominids; human beings,
modern
extinction, 28, 35, 36

F

facial expressions, 9
farming, 81
fat, 84
fetuses, 17, 34
fight-or-flight response, 15
fingers, 11–12, 37
fire, 63, 65
footprints, 50–53
fossils (about), 32, 45, 48, 75
fruit flies, 29
fur. *See* hair

G

generations, 24, 27, 29
geologists, 46–47, 54
germs, 27–28, 88
gestures, 40, 60
Gigantopithecus, 66–67
goose bumps, 13–14
gorillas, 16, 60

H

hair, 13, 16–17, 24–26
hares, 24–26
Hill, Andrew, 50
hominids, 39–44, 48–51,
55–67, 70–85, 90–91. *See also*
specific species
Homo antecessor, 67, 91
Homo erectus, 41, 63–66,
73–74, 91
Homo ergaster, 90–91
Homo habilis, 56, 62, 74, 90
Homo heidelbergensis, 67, 91
Homo rudolfensis, 90
Homo sapiens genus, 41, 72
Homo sapiens sapiens, 41,
80–84, 89. *See also*
Cro-Magnons; human beings,
modern; Neanderthals

horses, 32
human beings, modern, 80–89
  emotions, 17–18, 77
  evolution of, 6, 21, 23, 33, 39–40, 67, 80–81, 90–91
    See also Cro-Magnons; hominids; Neanderthals
  future evolution, 82, 86–89
  physical characteristics, 7–13, 16–17, 19–20, 33, 41, 62, 71, 84–85, 91
  population, 81–82
  races/skin color, 49, 82–83, 86
  variety, 43
  vestiges, 7–8, 10–11, 13, 15, 19
human beings, pre-modern. *See* Cro-Magnons; Neanderthals
hunting, 59, 64–65, 75
hypoglossal nerve, 66

ice ages, 36
Inherit the Wind, 73
insects, 27, 29, 34, 88
islands, 85

jaws, 33, 56, 71
jewelry, 12, 75, 79
Julie of the Wolves (George), 10

knuckle walking, 51

language, 7, 65–66, 73
Lascaux cave paintings, 77
Leakey family, 74
leg bones, 49, 90
life span, 82
linguistic roots, 7

love, 77
Lucy. *See Australopithecus afarensis*

maps, 61, 63, 71
Micronesia, 88
moles, 34
movies, 44, 73
museums, 92
mutations, 26, 28
Mysteries of Mankind, 73

natural selection, 24, 26. *See also* survival of the fittest
Neanderthals, 70–75, 77, 91
neighborhoods, 58, 59
nutcracker man. *See Australopithecus boisei*

One Million Years B.C., 73
Origin of Species, The (C. Darwin), 35
Origins Reconsidered (R. Leakey), 74
ostriches, 8, 33

paleoanthropologists, 48, 54, 74
paleontologists, 45, 54
pelvis, 48–49
penguins, 34
personality, 43
petroglyphs, 78
pigs, prehistoric, 58
Planet of the Apes, 73
poisons, 27
polar bears, 27
population growth, 82, 86
Protarchaeopteryx, 32
pulse, 15
pygmies, 85

rabbits. *See* hares
rats, 27
religion, 69
rhinarium, 10

salamanders, 34
scientific debate, 72
scientific thinking, 45, 48, 54, 72
Scopes Evolution Trial, 68, 73
Scopes, John, 68
sheep, prehistoric, 58
shelters, 76
size
  animal, 22–23, 32, 85
  hominid, 44, 48, 66–67, 70
  human, 70, 84–85
  See also brain
skin, 13, 49, 82–83, 86
skulls, 49, 56, 66, 71, 90–91
sleep, 19–20
smell, sense of, 10
smiles, 7, 9
snakes, 34
snarls, 9
Stone Age, 62, 90
subspecies, 30
sun, 27, 49, 82–83
survival of the fittest, 24, 35, 43, 82. *See also* natural selection

tails, 8
teeth
  canine, 7–9, 67
  hominid, 49, 56, 58, 62, 66–67, 90
  human, 7, 33–34, 62, 71, 86
  vestigial, 34
  Then and Now, 8, 32, 59, 62, 67, 82

Think About It!
  bacteria regeneration, 28
  Bigfoot today?, 67
  brain versus brawn, 42
  change, 37
  Darwin and his grandfather, 35
  discussion versus argument, 72
  hair, to have or not, 16
  neighborhood safety, 59
  saving the human race, 86
  science and the Bible, 69
  science detectives, 45
  scientific terms, 7
  welcoming gestures, 9
time line, 90–91
tools, 56, 59, 62, 64, 71, 75, 81, 90–91
Tyrannosaurus rex, 33

Ukraine, 76

Velociraptor, 32–33
vestiges, 8, 10–11, 13, 15–17, 31–32, 34
vitamin D, 83

walking upright, 38, 40, 49–51, 55, 72, 90
wasps, 34
water, 62
weapons, 59
Web sites, 59, 92
weight, 84–85
whales, 31, 34
wings, 8, 34
wisdom teeth, 33
wolves, 10, 23

zoologists/zoology, 7, 54

MORE GOOD BOOKS FROM WILLIAMSON PUBLISHING

KALEIDOSCOPE KIDS™ Books

Where Learning Meets Life
96 pages, two-color, fully
illustrated, 10 x 10,
$10.95, ages 6-12

Children's Book Council Notable Book
American Bookseller Pick of the Lists
PYRAMIDS!
**50 Hands-On Activities to Experience
Ancient Egypt**
by Avery Hart & Paul Mantell

American Bookseller Pick of the Lists
Children's Book Council Notable Book
KNIGHTS & CASTLES
**50 Hands-On Activities to Experience
the Middle Ages**
by Avery Hart & Paul Mantell

ANCIENT GREECE!
**40 Hands-On Activities to Experience
this Wondrous Age**
by Avery Hart & Paul Mantell

American Bookseller Pick of the Lists
MEXICO!
**40 Activities to Experience Mexico Past
and Present**
by Susan Milord

BRIDGES!
Amazing Structures to Design, Build & Test
by Carol A. Johmann and Elizabeth J. Rieth

GEOLOGY ROCKS!
50 Hands-on Activities to Explore the Earth
by Cindy Blobaum

VISIT OUR WEB SITE:

http://www.williamsonbooks.com
Or, call 800-234-8791 for catalog.

TO ORDER:

Williamson Books are available from your favorite bookseller,
or directly from Williamson Publishing.

Toll-free phone orders: 800-234-8791
E-mail orders to: **orders@williamsonbooks.com**
Visa or MasterCard accepted.

Or, send to:

Williamson Publishing
P.O. Box 185, Charlotte, Vermont 05445

Postage is **$3.20** for first book and **$.50** for each additional book.
Fully guaranteed.